Praise for *Breaking Good*

'A gripping and gritty depiction of the nightmare world of ice and drug crime. *Breaking Good* punches hard and shows no mercy. But Simon Fenech's compelling story is also a lesson for our times – no matter how bad things can get, there is always hope.'

Raphael Rowe, host of *Inside the World's Toughest Prisons*

'A compelling book on so many levels. The reader is drawn into the depths of Simon's desperation in order to appreciate the scale of his redemption. A great example of how social enterprises like Fruit2Work have the power to change and save lives.'

Geoff Harris, co-founder of Flight Centre

T0288309

BREAKING GOOD

BREAKING GOOD

SIMON FENECH
WITH NEIL BRAMWELL

echo

echo

Echo Publishing
An imprint of Bonnier Books UK
80–81 Wimpole Street
London W1G 9RE
www.echopublishing.com.au
www.bonnierbooks.co.uk

First published 2020

Cover design by Jo Hunt
Cover photography by Luka Kauzlaric
Page design and typesetting by Shaun Jury
Typeset in Bembo

Printed and bound in Australia by Griffin Press, part of Ovato.
Only wood grown from sustainable regrowth forests is used in the
manufacture of paper found in this book.

NATIONAL
LIBRARY
OF AUSTRALIA

A catalogue record for this book is available from the
National Library of Australia
ISBN: 9781760686468 (paperback)
ISBN: 9781760686741 (ebook)

echopublishingaustralia

echo_publishing

echo_publishing

To Victor – my brother, my rock

PROLOGUE

THE ROOM was a shithole. The congealed remains of takeaways were piled next to a mattress partially covered by a crumpled sleeping bag and a sweat-stained pillow. Ashtrays overflowed and the smell of unwashed men sat heavily in the air. Dirty crack pipes poked out from between the cushions of two tattered sofas and lay conspicuously on the floor. On the coffee table was a lighter, some clear Ziploc bags and a torn Magic Eraser sponge, while a set of digital scales sat on top of the open safe.

This was my office, my bedroom, my den – the hub of my dark existence.

In the corner, away from the window, I sat and stared at a 55-inch monitor. The screen was split into ten different feeds – all coming from the security cameras I'd recently installed inside and outside the factory and on the roads leading to my wrecking yard. Two mobile phones and a cordless landline lay inactive next to my laptop and printer. On a separate table was a two-way radio on a wavelength dedicated to wreckers and tow-truck operators. There were Post-It notes everywhere: *Ring Tyson*; *Troy H – $300*; a mobile phone number with no name attached. Open document binders spilled onto the shelving units and stacks of papers perched precariously on every available inch of desk.

I need to get on top of this, I thought, *but just not now*. One slow 360-degree swivel of the leather chair and I was back where I'd started – a restless inactivity. From downstairs came the soundtrack of a successful wrecking business; the clank of metal on metal as a stubborn car part finally budged; the screech of a demo saw chewing through a car door; the chatter of commercial radio; and the banter between the two lads working for me that day. This background noise was a rare reference point in a life without any order.

Axel, my pit bull terrier, nosed his way into the room and fussed around my ankles for attention. 'Not now, mate,' I said. 'Can't you see I'm busy?' His face dropped and he skulked down to the workshop floor to pester someone else. *Now, where was I?* I thumbed purposefully through a stack of papers, finding nothing that needed attention. *Check the phones, just in case.* No messages. *Send/receive emails.* Nothing new.

Any other small business owner would have taken the cue to wind down for the day and turn their thoughts to a bit of downtime: a night with their feet up in front of the telly; a meal out with the missus and kids; or maybe a few beers down the pub. But I hated downtime. It made me anxious. I had to be doing something, anything. *It's been an hour since my last hit. A quick puff and then I'll go downstairs and check on the boys.*

The kit was in the top drawer of my desk. A standard crack

pipe wasn't for me. A mate had warned me that standard pipes were a sure-fire way to fry your brain. I preferred the way the Asians smoked heroin – chasing the dragon. My kit was specialised, for a pro smoker: a homemade, self-blown glass pipe in the shape of a miniature saxophone, some hairdresser's aluminium foil and a modified lighter.

From the safe in the corner of the room I chose a decent-sized shard from my stash. There was probably about seven grams in the safe, with a street value of $2000, and there was about the same amount of cash, too. This rock would have weighed about three points (a point is a tenth of a gram), enough for a few big puffs. One point would have sufficed just a couple of months earlier. I ran some water from the sink in the washroom next door into the mouth of the sax, enough to fill the base an inch deep. I caught sight of myself in the mirror – dark rings around my eyes like a giant panda. That's what two or three hours of sleep a night does to you. *Go easy on it tonight*, I warned myself.

I tore off a section of foil. The stuff hairdressers used was much thicker and more manageable than regular cooking foil and transferred the heat more uniformly. Another trick was to use the smallest possible flame by taking the chrome cover off the top of a lighter and sticking a broken syringe needle into the jet to reduce the gas flow. This ensured the ice didn't cook. Often the flame had to be lit with a separate lighter and occasionally the modified lighters blew up. The foil was folded lengthways down the middle and a flat section was shaped at one end for the rock.

Holding the foil in one hand and the lighter in the other, with the mouthpiece of the sax between my lips, I fired the flame underneath the crystal. When it melted, I tilted the foil so that the liquid ran down the V-shaped funnel. As the liquid hit the cooler foil, the ice smoked and I chased the trail along the foil with the open end of the sax, sucking the fumes through the water. If there was enough left at the end – and enough air in my lungs – I could chase it back in the reverse direction. It was a wasteful way of smoking, because a lot of the ice vaporised, but it also burnt off some of the toxins. The water acted as filter for other impurities so that the smoke that I finally inhaled was much purer.

Whether it's your first ever meth experience, or the tenth of the day, there's always that *wow* moment when your hairs stand on end and every nerve in your body pulses with pleasure. But the addict needs more and more to reach those intense highs, which then don't last anywhere near as long. As always, this one briefly hit the spot. *Fuck paperwork and emails, I'm ready to take on the world.*

Anyone could see that business was booming. Racks of shelves, packed with salvaged parts, lined every wall of the workshop. Each item was meticulously colour-coded for make, model and year. Bigger items, such as full engines or doors, occasionally wheels, hung from the roof beams to create more space. Up the road was a paddock crammed with around two hundred cars, almost always Holdens and V8s in particular. Hoppers Crossing, a large suburb twenty-five kilometres south-west of Melbourne, next door to my home suburb of Werribee, was a Holden stronghold. People here took pride in their cars and were always on the lookout for that customised part which would improve performance or make their motor stand out from the crowd. My approach was simple – if I bought all the available cars, there'd be nothing left for the opposition. There was decent coin to be made and, although I was personally hurtling towards rock bottom, I somehow managed to run a good little business. The twenty-hour working days probably helped. But the exhaustion and numbness caused by my addiction meant that I was working hard, not working smart.

Dave, a young guy in his mid-twenties from Werribee, was different to a lot of the fellas who worked for me. He was clean and I trusted him not to steal from me. He kept his head down, his nose out of my business, picked up his wad of cash at the end of the week and never caused me any trouble. I didn't need to know whether he also signed on at Centrelink.

A new bloke, Billy, was sleeping in one of the other bedrooms upstairs while he sorted his shit out. He was an addict and basically worked for his next fix. I did plenty of deals like that. Perhaps I was seen as a soft touch because I often supplied ice on tick or sold to my regulars at nearly half the street value. But I was never short of buyers – one-point customers, two-point customers, one-gram customers. Even at this level of discount, dealing paid for my next stash, my own habit, enough for the boys who were working for me, and a free smoke for almost anyone who dropped by. More often than not, these guys would then introduce a mate at some point.

'All good down here?' I asked Dave, as Axel stirred from his afternoon nap and trotted after me through to the work area.

'Yeah, mate. I'll have finished stripping this one in half an hour. Okay if I knock off after that?'

'No worries. How's Billy working out?' I asked under my breath.

'So so,' said Dave. 'Bit weird, but he knows his way around a car.'

Meth feeds paranoia, so I always kept a close eye on the new blokes. This Billy fella had been working for me for about two weeks and nothing was missing, so far. Most guys started off not wanting to bite the hand that was feeding them their ice, until they became desperate.

I did have a couple of good reasons to be paranoid. Three months earlier, a team of cops in divi vans and unmarked cars had raided the joint the day before my mum's funeral. They were certain I was running a chop shop for stripping stolen cars. You bet your life the bastards timed it deliberately, when I was deranged with grief and smoking anything I could lay my hands on. On that occasion I managed to hide my main stash in the nick of time and their search for stolen cars was fruitless. They were pissed off and it was obvious they'd be back with a vengeance. Also, there'd been a couple of break-ins at the factory and also in the paddock. A week ago my guard dog, a staffy–pit bull cross called Black Betty, had been beaten senseless when someone broke into the paddock. So I was on high alert, constantly looking over my shoulder.

Although there was another security camera feed in the downstairs office, which doubled as a lounge area, I went back upstairs and settled behind the desk just as an olive-green Holden Commodore pulled up. It wasn't unusual for new customers to arrive unannounced so there was no immediate cause for alarm, especially when I recognised two of the three blokes who got out the car.

The first was a mate of Dave's, a burly guy with a shaggy red beard, wearing a hillbilly black-and-white flannelette shirt, jeans and work boots. Red was a Holden fanatic and a regular at the factory, so I often sold him parts at just a shade above cost. His son was into bikes and had brought a couple of his Harleys round to show me. Red had become something of a mate, but I was more wary of the second guy. He'd been released from prison about two weeks earlier with a reputation much bigger than his skinny frame. Stevo had been sent down for a series of knife attacks and was a mad bastard by all accounts. Word was out that he'd been trying to form his own gang and Red wanted to be a part of it. When Red asked me if I could help Stevo out with some work, I was willing to give him a chance. I even loaned him one of the scrap cars, which still had a couple of months rego remaining, so that he could travel to and from work. But on the day he was due to start there was no sign of him. *The car's only worth $200,* I thought. *No point tracking him down for that.* I should've known never to turn a blind eye when someone was taking the piss. It's seen as a sign of weakness. I didn't mention it when I went downstairs to meet them.

'G'day Red, what's going on, mate?' I asked cheerily.

'Not much, bro. I'm looking for a black centre console for a Berlina. Got one in stock?'

'Think so,' I replied. 'Just let me check upstairs on the computer. Be down in a minute.' I bounded back upstairs past Stevo, who avoided eye contact, and the third guy, their driver. He looked Eastern European, of medium build with long, scruffy hair. His body language was edgy, hostile even. Both he and Stevo were dressed in the standard urban uniform — black hoodie, tracky dacks and the latest kicks. The driver wore a thick gold chain around his neck.

Sure enough, a couple of consoles were in stock, so I made a note of their code and went back downstairs. Red had wandered through the open roller door, which was chained off for staff access only, to talk to Dave. There was nothing unusual about that, but the other two had followed him inside and were hanging around one of the wall racks, near where the forklift was parked. Something felt weird as I approached them to locate the part.

'Where's the money?' said the driver with a quiet menace that prevented the guys at the back of the factory from hearing.

'Eh? What money?'

'You owe us two grand,' he said.

'The fuck are you talking about? I don't owe nobody no fucking money.'

Without another word the driver pulled a pistol out of the double pocket at the front of his hoodie and fired two shots. Fury fogged my brain. *You fucking dog, nobody pulls a gun at me!* He was about five metres away and as I lunged towards him, he aimed the gun at me again and pulled the trigger. The thing jammed and, panicking, he threw it to Stevo. I charged at the driver, grabbing him around his waist and wrestling him towards the roller door until he fell backwards. I landed on top of him, lashing out like a madman. There was blood everywhere, a lot coming from his face because I got in a couple of good punches. Out of the corner of my eye I spotted the shovel that I kept handy to clean up Axel's shit. As I staggered towards it, I realised that one leg of my overalls was torn and wet. A bullet had passed through my thigh, but in that pure rage I hadn't even noticed. The combination of ice and the adrenaline masked the pain.

I heard a cry behind me and turned to see Axel, who'd sprinted the length of the factory, launch himself at the driver and sink his teeth into the prick's shoulder. I would never have guessed that my dog, everybody's best mate, had it in him. But he'd transformed into a ferocious killing machine and would have torn the driver limb from limb had he not seen me stumbling towards them with the shovel in hand. Axel must have thought he was in for a beating because he let go and bolted, just as I smashed the driver across the head. Next I sensed someone coming at me from behind and turned to see Stevo holding a homemade shiv, a sharpened metal file with tape wrapped around the handle. He hesitated, weighing up his chances. In that split second the driver struggled back onto his feet and pulled a twelve-inch kitchen knife from the sleeve of his hoodie. He plunged the blade into the flesh at the back of my neck. Reality was starting to become fuzzy and the second slash almost seemed to happen in slow motion. Then there was a third thrust, which felt completely different. The tip of the blade landed in one of the links of my thick, silver necklace and, instead of slicing into my flesh, just yanked the chain tight around my neck. But I was still barely aware that I'd been stabbed at all.

'Leave him!' Stevo yelled. 'He's fucked up.'

'I'll show you who's fucked up,' I said, catching my breath.

'No, seriously, you need to get yourself to hospital,' Stevo said. 'You're bleeding heaps.'

What the fuck is he on about? The leg wound's just a graze. Then I touched the back of my neck and realised that my T-shirt was wet. But I still felt no pain and had no awareness that I was wounded. When I saw the driver making a dash for his car, self-preservation was the last thing on my mind. I was going to make this fucker pay.

By the time I reached my car, a Holden Clubsport that was

my pride and joy, the olive-green Commodore was at the bottom of the driveway and heading for the Princes Freeway slip road. It was afternoon rush hour and the traffic was backing up. If he'd joined the queue, he knew I would've chased after him on foot and caught him. So he swung the Commodore onto the grass verge and flew down the inside of the stationary vehicles. I had no option but to follow. Although the traffic was heavy it was moving and I quickly caught up, close enough to slam into his rear. I was still not thinking clearly, but probably wanted to spin him ninety degrees to a standstill. If I'd clipped him harder, it could have caused carnage, but he managed to keep control and speed away again. Using the inside lane, I pulled alongside. I wanted him to see the whites of my eyes, to witness the monster he'd unleashed. But he fixed his stare on the road ahead. Suddenly, there was a slow-moving truck in front of me and I had to swerve onto the hard shoulder to avoid ploughing into the back of it.

As I skidded to a stop, I became aware that my racing bucket seat was soaking wet. *Fuck me, this interior is ruined.* Almost as an afterthought, I touched the back of my neck again, and everything felt wrong up there. *Shit, I do need a hospital, and fast.* By then I was starting to feel really dizzy. I was about five kilometres away from Werribee Mercy Hospital. It was too risky to re-join the traffic so I put my foot down and sped down the hard shoulder, cutting straight across the next exit and onto the Princes Freeway.

At the hospital I pulled in at the entrance to the Emergency Department and stopped where the ambulances offload their patients. Gently, I eased myself out of the car and lurched, hunched like a wounded bear, through two sets of automatic doors and into the reception area. The queue to the receptionist's window was ten-deep and there wasn't an empty seat in the waiting room. But, at the next window along, a nurse was catching up on some paperwork behind a 'position closed' sign. As I stumbled through the rows of waiting patients and their families, I could hear gasps of horror. One poor kid screamed at the top of her voice. It must've looked like someone had tipped a bucket of blood over my head. When I reached the closed window I slumped on the counter. The nurse looked up from her work and almost retched.

'What happened?' she asked, petrified.

'I dropped a big piece of steel on my neck and I'm bleeding bad.'

'Turn around and let me look. Pull up your T-shirt.'

'I will, but maybe ask everyone else to look away.'

'Look, you're in a bad way, just do it.'

I turned round, undid the straps on my overalls and reached behind to peel away the shreds of T-shirt. Blood spurted from my back like an artery had been cut. Droplets hit the window, the counter and the face of the traumatised nurse.

'Code red, code red!' she shrieked.

Within seconds a team of nurses descended on what must have looked like the scene of a grisly massacre. They bundled me onto a trolley and out of the reception area, straight to a resuscitation bay. I was rolled onto my stomach and told not to move a muscle. The rest of my clothes were cut off as intravenous drips were inserted and wires attached to my arms and legs. I'm not sure if I was conscious the whole time but I do remember hearing a copper enter the room and, scoffing, telling the medics that this was no work accident, as if they didn't already know.

A young male doctor bent over me and whispered, 'You're going to be all right, mate, you're going to pull through.'

Nah, mate. You're wrong — I'm fucked. I'm gonna die. My poor kids. What's going to happen to my kids?

CHAPTER **ONE**

'REPRESENTING AUSTRALIA . . . we all know him as The Hoppers Crossing Hitman . . . the reigning Australian kickboxing champion . . . Simon Fenech!' The announcer was drowned out by the cheers of hundreds of fans crammed into the Knox Basketball Stadium on the outskirts of Melbourne. Foxtel were televising this one-off 'Ashes Series' – Australia versus Great Britain – and the cameras tracked me as I danced around the ring, kicking shadows and punching spotlight beams. My ponytail slapped angrily against the muscles of my back, which glistened like polished mahogany. I was confident. Perhaps over-confident.

For the previous six months I had trained morning and night, seven days a week, and was as fit and strong and ripped as I had ever been. People were calling me the Raging Bull, after Jake LaMotta, the legendary boxer played by Robert de Niro in the famous film. I had the same ruthless instinct. When I sensed weakness in an opponent I went in for the kill. Being short and stocky, I struggled to land kicks above my taller opponents' waists. So my style was all about upper body strength and the speed of my fists. I could string together furious combinations of punches that sent opponents cowering to the ropes.

My trainer, Ivon Reffo, told me to pace myself, to use cunning as well as brute force. 'Feel your way into the fight,' he urged. 'Work out his weakness. Wear him down. You don't have to win every fight in the first two rounds.' Not my style.

My previous bout, for the Australian amateur title, had followed the usual pattern. Romolo 'The Wild Samoan' Pio, an unpredictable fighter who had been around the circuit for years, came at me hard. But the only form of defence I knew was attack. The Samoan was moaning on the canvas within two rounds. It was such a proud moment for me, but even more so for my dad, Joe. All of a sudden, his slightly chubby adolescent son, who could never kick a footy or hit a cricket ball, was a champion sportsman. That title belt lived in his car for weeks as he showed it off to all his Maltese mates in Sunshine, a suburb in Melbourne's west. Then, when the DVD of the fight dropped though the letterbox a couple of weeks later, he visited them all again. 'That's my boy, Simon, a *chumpion*,' he boasted, in his thick Maltese accent. 'Can you believe it?'

The offers came flooding in after that win, but nobody was more surprised than me when the promoter rang to ask if I wanted to challenge for the Commonwealth title as the main undercard fight of the Ashes series. The reigning champion was Sheldon Schutzler, a South African who was allowed to represent Great Britain because he lived in Belfast.

Ivon was nervous. 'We know nothing about this guy,' he

warned. 'The Commonwealth champion is going to be no mug. It's too soon for you. Defend your Australian title first.'

'Are you fucking serious? If I win this fight, I'll have a crack at the world amateur title. I don't care if this guy is a fucking monster, he's going down.'

It was common practice to send your opponent a compilation of your fights, to help them prepare. But we got nothing out of Belfast, so I had no idea what to expect from Schutzler. Still, as I warmed up backstage, there didn't seem any need to worry. The Aussies had won every one of the first five bouts and we seemed unbeatable.

'From Great Britain . . . the reigning Commonwealth titleholder . . . Sheldon Schutzler!' announced the emcee. *Fucker doesn't even have a nickname*, was my first thought. *Fuck me sideways*, was my second, as Schutzler clomped into the ring. Remember Ivan Drago, the Russian who fought Rocky Balboa in *Rocky IV*? Well, this guy made Drago look like a dwarf. But there was nowhere to hide. Too many people were relying on me: the TV audience at home; the supporters in the arena; the rest of the Australian team; Ivon, my trainer; and, most of all, my old man. No way could I let him down. I glanced over at Dad's usual spot in the front row, so near to my corner that he could bark instructions to my team and insults at the referee. Sure enough, there he was, calmly holding my wife Vicky's hand, who looked more nervous than me. Dad glanced up at me and winked, as if to say, 'Son, kick his arse.'

Within minutes I was staring into Dad's eyes again, flat on my back on the massage table in the changing room, blood pouring from my nose. The room was spinning.

'Simon? Simon? Look at me. How many fingers?' Dad asked, unable to disguise the worry in his voice.

'Yeah, fat fingers,' I muttered. Everyone looked worried. What the hell was I talking about? 'What round is it?' I asked.

'Your last round, son,' he replied, with authority. 'He got you good. That bastard was big. We'll talk about it more when we get home, but Vicky is in tears out there. So I'm telling you, make this your last fight. There's no need for it. You don't have to prove anything to me or anyone else.' Even half-gaga I realised that, if my pain was causing him pain, I would have to think carefully about ever fighting again.

***

LIKE MOST Maltese, my old man knew the value of a dollar when he arrived in Australia in the late 1950s. His own father was killed during the Siege of Malta in World War II, when the limestone church he was building was bombed by the Italian and German air forces. His mother had died giving birth to twins when Dad was a young boy and so, after his father's death, he became the head of the family while just a teenager. Even before his compulsory stint of National Service in the British Navy, he travelled to Manchester in England to work in the cotton mills and send money home to his stepmother. Back in Malta, where he met my mum, Margaret, life was tough and Australia promised new prosperity for a young family. My parents migrated and settled in the suburb of West Sunshine, in Melbourne's working-class west.

Dad found work as a metal buyer and by the time I was five,

he'd saved enough money to buy a 25-acre plot of land between Melton and Werribee. There, he built our home, several sheds and a granny flat. It was a big deal for a man of such humble origins. My brothers, Vic and Dave, were a lot older than me at sixteen and thirteen respectively – the telly must've broken nine months before I arrived – so I was effectively brought up as an only child. Dad and I were inseparable. Every night when he came home from work, we'd spend hours looking after the animals together. We kept every creature under the sun: pigs, ducks, goats, peacocks, sheep, cows, horses, pheasants, rabbits – lots of rabbits, a popular delicacy in Malta – and Mum cooked a delicious rabbit stew. When I showed an interest in breeding finches and parrots, Dad bought me the most expensive birds. I loved goats and Anglo-Nubians, the breed with the long floppy ears, in particular. Dad found one for sale in the *Weekly Times* and had it shipped from interstate. Nothing but the best was good enough for Simon. This was his way of making up for the fact that we lived in the middle of nowhere and visits from my mates were rare.

The farm was no place for the faint-hearted and I grew up quickly. It would not be unusual for me to feed our pet lambs with milk from a bottle before I left for school, only to come home and find them skinned and hung, ready for the dinner table. My dog, Kadida, a bull terrier–greyhound cross, was a fast, powerful killing machine. I needed to be first up in the morning to wash any blood from Kadida's mouth in case he'd escaped from his pen during the night and killed one of Dad's sheep. 'Those bastard foxes again,' I muttered, to throw him off the scent. Dad would sit on the porch for hours in the evenings with his shotgun, but the foxes never came.

Dad was an encyclopaedia of hands-on skills, like how to build pens, skin rabbits, change the oil of a tractor, or knowing how long it would take for an egg to hatch in the incubator compared to under a breeding hen. Once a year we took the 8 a.m. train to the Royal Melbourne Show to be the first to wander through the poultry pavilion. If any of the prize ducks, chickens or guinea fowls had laid an egg it would disappear into our backpack so that we could hatch the best breeding birds back home. Always resourceful, Dad's work was never done and his thickset body was tireless. His hands were the size of buckets and his fingers as thick as the carrots we grew. Although his practical advice was invaluable, he used our time together for something far more precious. He taught me how to be a good man.

'If you remember just one thing that I tell you, Simon, remember this,' he said, one sultry evening as we leant on the fence, watching the cows lazily take their feed. 'If you do right by people, they will do right by you. Family is everything. A Maltese family will never let you down. Every cent I make is for you, your brothers and your mother. Look at this house, this farm, this land. It all cost money and money comes from hard work. And without money, son, you are nothing in this world.' No young boy could ever have been so in awe of his father.

Then, one night when I was about ten years old, I woke to hear Dad pacing around the kitchen table, groaning.

'It's probably just your indigestion, love,' Mum told him. 'Drink a glass of milk and go back to bed.'

'Mum, he doesn't look right,' I said. 'He's almost grey. We should call an ambulance.'

Dad hated doctors but he nodded weakly. As Mum rang the

emergency services and tried to describe our location, I covered Dad with a blanket and held his hand tightly. It took half an hour for the ambulance to arrive and, the instant the first paramedic set foot through the front door, Dad suffered a massive heart attack. I could barely watch as my rock, suddenly so helpless and frail, had an intravenous drip inserted into his arm, was wired up to various monitors and bundled onto a stretcher. As the crew lifted him into the ambulance one of the machines stopped beeping and emitted that dreaded high-pitch whine.

'He's flat-lining!' yelled the female paramedic. 'Get the defibrillator ready. You two, stand back.'

Mum and I watched in horror as the pads were placed on his chest and the first jolt did nothing. Neither did the second.

'My husband!' wailed Mum, fearing the worst.

'Try one more,' said the paramedic in charge. Agonising moments after that final shock, a faint beep was heard and the monitor's trace hinted at renewed hope.

We were allowed to travel to hospital with him, but his condition remained so serious that halfway along one of the dark country lanes we stopped and were met by a mobile intensive care ambulance. While Dad was being transferred between vehicles he flat-lined again. The faces of the ambos betrayed their fears. It took three more shocks to revive Dad's heartbeat – and that's a lot of trauma for any heart to withstand. As the smaller intensive care ambulance pulled away without us, we didn't know whether he would even make it to hospital. Mum was in floods of tears and I was too shocked to realise that, for a few horrible seconds, I had watched my father die.

Although he pulled through, doctors said that his heart would not survive another attack and advised him to retire from his full-time job. At the age of fifty he was put out to pasture, which must have been torture for such a proud man, although the upside for me was that we got to spend even more time together. He continued to make a dollar here and there by selling our animals or veggies but I could tell he felt incomplete without a job, although he never once moaned. It made me doubly determined to restore his pride through seeing me succeed.

At the age of fifteen I quit school, where I was a distraction to the kids who wanted to learn, and went to work for my elder brother, Vic, who managed an electrical goods store. Here was another level-headed man who would do anything for anyone. Nobody had a bad word to say about him. Vic was another great role model for me and, during my five years at the company, taught me the value of treating your colleagues and employees with respect. But having spent so much of my youth outdoors, I didn't like being cooped up inside a shop. Dad loaned me $7000 to buy a furniture van with a hydraulic tail lift and, working for a taxi truck company and doing private removals at the weekend, I paid him back within seven weeks – and saved another $7000. It was hard yakka, but good hard yakka.

A driver's licence meant freedom to spread my wings. I went on regular hunting trips with a couple of older mates: Frank, the son of one of our nearest neighbours from a farm about three or four kilometres away, and Fabio. These guys introduced me to kickboxing when I was that chubby seventeen year old through Ivon, a family man who worked as a carpenter by day and a trainer by night. His twin motivations were his love of the sport and a desire to see his fighters succeed. The club was based in a double-storey garage at the back of Ivon's house. It consisted of a dirt floor, a few pairs of tattered gloves, a couple of shabby punching bags and a makeshift ring that Ivon had knocked together. We roasted in there on hot summer days. It smelt so bad that flies turned back at the door. For a long time I was the human punching bag for the older fellas. But as the puppy fat melted away, a solid physique emerged: shoulders as wide as an ironing board and legs as thick as tree trunks.

While the boys went clubbing at the weekend in Melbourne's CBD, I would put in an extra training session with Ivon on a Saturday afternoon. The one-on-one time was invaluable and after a year I was ready for my first bout against another Maltese fighter, Tony Mizzi, who was much more experienced. I was expecting nothing more than a hard spar but it turned into an all-out slugging match. Deep into the fourth round this animal had me trapped against the ropes. His kicks to my side bent me double and he followed up with a barrage of solid hits to my head. All I could do was curl into a defensive crouch and hope the bell would allow me to regroup. But before the end of the round came, the ref called 'break'.

'I'm okay,' I gasped. 'Don't stop the fight.'

'I'm not stopping the fight!' he shouted. 'I'm stopping that idiot trying to get in the ring!' I looked up to see my old man clambering over the ropes. It took Ivon and Frank, one grabbing his legs and the other pinning his arms to his sides, to wrestle him away.

'You fuck with my boy, you fuck with me!' Dad shouted, struggling to break free. The crowd loved it, and was probably disappointed when the real fight was allowed to continue. The ref didn't dare award the victory to the other bloke and called it a draw.

That night the boys took me into the CBD to celebrate at one of their regular haunts. Fabio, a handsome Italian rooster, spotted a girl he'd tried to impress the previous week: a gorgeous, slim blonde with a smile like a dancefloor strobe. But she was smiling my way, not Fabio's. Vicky was a hairdresser and two years older than me and displayed an innocent lust for life that I'd never encountered before. My parents fell for her as heavily as I did, even though Mum had previously told me to 'marry a good Maltese girl'.

Exactly one year after our first date at a Chinese restaurant in Werribee called Master Wok, Vicky drove us back there to celebrate our anniversary. After we'd eaten, we went out to the carpark but, to Vicky's horror, her car was gone.

'Look, let's deal with it in the morning,' I said. 'There's nothing anyone can do this late at night.'

'No, Simon, we have to go to the cops now,' she insisted.

'Okay, maybe that limo over there will give us a lift.' I walked across the car park, tapped on the window and loudly explained the situation to the driver. Of course, unbeknown to Vicky, I'd given him her spare car keys earlier that afternoon.

'Are you for real? I can't believe we are going to the police station in a stretch limo,' Vicky said as she climbed in. She was horrified when I helped myself to a couple of glasses of champagne. 'Simon! He can see through that blacked-out screen, you know,' she said and giggled. It was only when the limo dropped us off at the Hilton Hotel that the penny dropped.

Tears trickled down her face as I went down on one knee and, after saying 'yes', Vicky pinned me to the bed.

'Hang on . . . one second . . .' I gasped, coming up for air. 'There's something I have to do first.' I'm not sure what Vicky was expecting, but she definitely wasn't expecting me to interrupt our moment of passion to phone my dad.

We were married one year later and I phoned my old man when we arrived at our honeymoon suite in Malaysia, also when I won a lucrative delivery contract for Betta Electrical, and again when we bought our first home on a third of an acre plot in Hoppers Crossing. Nothing made me happier than hearing the intense pride in Dad's voice whenever I told him any good news. And it was only ever good news for such a very long time.

***

IT TOOK me weeks to fully recover from the flogging at the hands of Sheldon Schutzler. The scars healed, the swelling sub-sided and the concussion disappeared, but Dad's plea to stop fighting wouldn't leave my head. On one hand, it made so much sense. Married life was blissful and I was earning good money, paying chunks off the home loan. This was the life Dad dreamt of for me. Why risk it all for a dangerous sport that didn't pay the bills? On the other hand, I had finally found something I was good at. Nothing in my life came close to matching the surge of adrenaline during a fight. Even training was like a drug. Surely I could put one beating behind me and go on to bigger and better things? There was never any thought of turning pro, but a shot at a world title was within my grasp.

The dilemma was soon resolved in the cruellest of ways. Dad had been complaining for some time of pains in his back and stomach. 'The back pain's just the slipped disc flaring up, and the pain in your stomach is the old ulcer,' our family GP, a bit of a dinosaur, flippantly stated before sending Dad home with a couple of prescriptions. The pain intensified and we took him to a new GP, Dr Alan Underwood, a young country bloke who wore his Blundstones to work and spoke to my old man as an equal.

'Had a piss or shit today, Joe? No? Okay then, I reckon we'd better book you in for some scans straight away.' Those scans revealed a tumour the size of a tennis ball in his pancreas. 'Look, I'm not going to lie to you,' Dr Underwood said. 'This is one of the most aggressive cancers there is. But we'll start you on radiation therapy straight away and all we can do is hope for the best.'

Dad had already proved he was invincible. Shit, he'd actually died twice. But somehow this sounded far more ominous. I was in a daze as I drove him home from the doctor's surgery to deliver the news to Mum, who ran to the bedroom and collapsed in tears. 'It's not the end of the world,' Dad stated calmly. 'There's life in this old bastard yet. So let's just see if we can't beat this thing before we go getting all upset.'

From that moment there was only one fight I could focus on. Kickboxing didn't enter my head. I devoted every spare minute to being the best son possible. I mowed the paddocks once a week, fed the animals after finishing work, and drove Dad to every appointment for his radiation. But the treatment knocked the shit out of him. He retreated within himself and refused to talk about the disease or his treatment. The farm was also becoming a burden, so we sold it at a giveaway price and moved Dad and Mum into a newer, smaller house in the suburbs, just around the corner from our home. It was a relief not having to maintain the farm and, for a while, the twinkle returned to his eyes.

Then, when Vicky and I told him that he was going to be a grandparent again, all his stifled emotions erupted in a torrent of tears and a hug which spoke volumes without the need for words. *Son, you never stop making me proud*, his embrace told me.

***

IT WAS no surprise when the doctor delivered the results of the radiation treatment. The cancer had spread, and Dad had just a few months to live. 'Death is part of life,' he told me in the car, words I hear clearly to this day. 'What can you do, eh?'

What can you do? What do you mean 'what can you do?' My blood was boiling. Here was a good Catholic man, faithful all his life to one woman, who didn't drink or smoke, never gambled, worked like a machine, and was always there for his family. And he deserves this? Well, fuck this. Fuck everyone and everything. That's what I can do. On the outside I tried to remain composed and supportive, but something shattered inside me that day.

My anger needed an outlet, and that release was fighting. I threw myself back into my training with a phenomenal intensity. When I couldn't run another metre, I ran on. When there were no punches left, I punched harder. Ivon didn't recognise this new fighter in his stable and quickly lined up a fight for the South Pacific title against an Aussie bloke called Brent Porter. I actually felt sorry for this guy. He wouldn't know what'd hit him. I felt different, almost savage. And I needed a new look to reflect this transformation. Vicky shaved a clean 'V' into the back of my head. Then I did something that would have been unthinkable just months previously. I got a Celtic tribal pattern tattooed on my arm. There was no significance, it just looked wild. I was careful always to wear long-sleeve shirts when visiting Dad, who'd self-combusted when my brother, Dave, came home with a few tatts. Everything about my preparation was different. I could even endure the three-week sex ban. I was saving every ounce of testosterone for the ring.

The fight was over in one and a half rounds. Porter was a mess. I hadn't told Dad about the contest, as I didn't want him to worry. Instead, I dropped by their new house and casually placed my title belt on the kitchen table.

'What you brought this for?' he asked. 'I seen it already.'

'Not this one, you haven't.'

'South Pacific Champion? Are you fighting again? And what's this say...?' He'd noticed the inscription on the huge bronze buckle: *For my dad, Joe. My hero. My world.* He swallowed hard and dropped his head into his hands, his shoulders heaving gently. Dad only cried in that way one more time, when Vicky and I presented him with our son, Jake.

A year earlier Jake would've fitted in the palm of one of Dad's enormous hands. Now, with his body weight almost halved, he appeared more fragile than the baby. It was inevitable that he only had a few more weeks at home. When the time came for him to be moved into hospital, carrying him to the car was heartbreaking. I knew that he would never return. All three sons spent hours at his bedside, but Mum found it all too traumatic and stuck to regular visiting hours. For much of the time he was too sedated to realise we were there, but I was honoured to provide any comfort I could offer by keeping him company long into the night and washing him when his body lost control. It would've been the ultimate indignity for my old man to have been bathed by the young nurses.

Two weeks into his stay in hospital, I somehow sensed that he was calling for me in the middle of the night. I drove to the hospital and entered his private room to find him barely conscious and breathing in irregular, rasping pants. The room stank and he'd obviously just had an accident, so I cleaned him up. I'm not sure he knew that I was there, but he didn't need to express his pain in words or sounds or expressions. It was all too obvious. Back on the farm, there was never any hesitation to put a suffering animal out of its misery. The authorities would probably have prosecuted us if we'd left an animal in that much pain.

Why is it any different for humans? I asked myself. *Isn't it cruel to let a loved one suffer?* As I stroked his hand and wept into his sheets, I couldn't get the scene from the film *One Flew Over the Cuckoo's Nest* out of my head, when Chief discovered that Jack Nicholson's McMurphy character had undergone a lobotomy and smothered him with a pillow. *Was that not the ultimate act of love? Nobody will ever know if I send Dad to a better place right now. Isn't this the merciful, dutiful, beautiful thing for a son to do?* I lifted Dad's head slightly, took one of his pillows away, and carefully lowered his head. Straining hard to stifle my sobs, I leant over to kiss him on the forehead. I placed the pillow over his face and my hand over the pillow, covering his nose and mouth. Then, without warning, Dad lifted his hand and grabbed my forearm.

His eyes didn't open, no sound escaped his lips. He just held onto my arm with all his remaining strength. Was it resistance? Or was it his blessing? I couldn't take the risk and tucked the pillow back under his head.

I'll never know Dad's intention that night, but I do know this: when Joseph Fenech died a few days later, part of Simon Fenech died with him.

CHAPTER **TWO**

THE HARLEY was my pride and joy, a jaw-dropping, jet-black beast of a machine: snarling 1340 cc twin engine; cushion-soft seats studded along the seams with a perch for my girl at the back; three headlights beneath a tasselled, leather tool bag for spanners and Allen keys; sturdy, polished leather saddle bags at each side; shiny running footboards and highway pegs; and a gleaming chrome crankcase that you could shave in. The Heritage Softail was a classic bikie's bike. For the gangs, these machines represented muscle and defiance. For me, it meant release from the growing monotony of family life. A Sunday afternoon at home with Vicky and Jake was no longer enough. I craved the freedom of the open road, the wind on my face, and the bone-shuddering echo of the engine's growl as I pinned the throttle in a tunnel or under a bridge.

Okay, it was a status symbol, too. The number plate – ENV1 – was a giveaway. Money had continued to roll in over the two or three years since Dad's death. Betta Electrical booked me for between twelve and twenty deliveries a day, at $35 a job. But most of their customers also wanted their old washing machines and fridges taken away. I charged them $30 for that service, cash in hand. Then I sold these washers and fridges on to a couple of repairers for anything up to $70, depending on the age of the machine. If the appliances were still in working order, I listed them in the *Trading Post* for around $100. I was raking it in, legitimately, and then using the redraw facility on our house to buy my toys. The Harley set me back $24,000. When I started earning more cash as a bouncer in the evenings and I was working all hours God sent, it was actually rare for me to fire her up. It was even rarer for Vicky, who was 100 per cent focused on Jake, to come along for a ride. She didn't begrudge me a bit of extravagance, though, because I was a good, hard-working, level-headed provider. She trusted me with our finances. She didn't even whinge when I imported a Chevy Silverado Ute from Texas – ENVI 2 – for around $70,000. The Chevy was the only one of its kind in Australia, with a stepside rear and external wheel arches – a ute to out-ute all utes. But I was smart and bought Vicky a brand new Holden SS Commodore – ENVI SS – so that she didn't feel left out.

'What's with all this *envy* stuff?' asked Vic, who'd dropped by one weekend for a barbecue and a few beers. 'It's not like you. You used to be a lot more humble, even when you were doing well at the kickboxing. Don't go forgetting where you come from.'

'Aw, come on, Vic,' I said. 'It's just a bit of fun. What's the point of working my arse off just to pay off the mortgage and then buy a bigger house and work even harder to pay that off?

Life's for living. Fuck, nobody knows more than I do just how easily it can be taken away. Remember the day on the beach? That changed me, brother. You might not realise how much.'

Vic fell silent. He knew which day I meant. I'd jumped at the chance a few years back when a mate invited me down to Werribee South to muck around on his jet ski. I must have been around twenty. It was a scorcher and the beach was packed with local families. When it was my turn on the jet ski, I carefully weaved my way from the sand ramp away from the bathers towards the deeper water. I noticed a couple of young lads, aged around ten and possibly twins, sitting facing each other in a blow-up dinghy, giggling away as the waves tossed them around. Farther out in the deeper, darker water, I started to lose my nerve. This was shark territory, and my toes were too near the surface for comfort. So I headed back towards shore. I noticed another jet ski hurtling along, parallel to the beach. *Dickhead's too near to the shore to be going at that speed*, I thought. As I approached the beach, I noticed that everyone in the water and on the beach seemed to freeze. Then, almost instantly, there was mayhem as all the bathers scrambled out of the water. *Shit, I was right, there is a shark. I need to scare it off.* I gunned the jet ski towards the beach and, when a short distance away, spotted the boys' blow-up dinghy. They were no longer upright, but slumped at either end. Pulling slowly closer, I could see the blood. I jumped off the jet ski and waded through the waist-deep water towards the inflatable as another bloke sprinted into the water from the beach.

'What the fuck happened here?' I yelled.

'That prick on the jet ski over there was riding backwards, sitting on the bonnet. He couldn't see where he was going. Ran right over the top of them and kept on going. Still probably doesn't know what he's done. I'm a paramedic. Pull the dinghy in then you grab that kid and I'll carry the other. Check his pulse, too.'

I grabbed the kid's wrist and felt a weak pulse. 'He's alive, just!' I shouted. As I hauled the boy out of the dinghy, I heard a sound that haunts me to this day – the animal howl of a mother who believed that she'd witnessed the death of her babies. Then came another scream of pure rage – it was the father charging into the water towards the jet skier. The jet skier jumped off his jet ski and dropped beneath the surface. After around twenty seconds he resurfaced to gasp for air and let out his own pitiful wail as onlookers struggled to keep the father from tearing him limb from limb.

An ambulance soon arrived. Helicopters circled overhead and the police led the jet skier away. It didn't look good for the nine year old that the paramedic had rescued. The jet ski had split open the back of his head. His eleven-year-old brother, who I'd carried, had been hit under the chin and was bleeding from his nose and ears, but didn't appear to be as badly hurt. There was nothing more for me to do but pray as the ambulances drove away from beach and the police took statements.

I was still traumatised the next day when I heard on the news that only the younger kid had survived. Perhaps his brother's final breaths had been taken in my arms. I couldn't imagine how that family would ever recover. Such wounds can never truly heal. In fact, both parents recognised me from working at Vic's store at the shopping centre and often sought me out over the next few months to thank me for trying to save their son, but mainly to offload their grief. My brother Vic had seen first-hand the lasting effects of that day's events, and he was acutely aware how Dad's death had left its own deep emotional scar.

'I'm not saying don't make the most of life,' he said now. 'This is about the *way* you're living your life. Could you have imagined the old man driving round in a flash car or riding a Harley? Dad wasn't a show-off. Just the opposite. He was all about modesty, humility, dignity. Remember his last words to you – to do right by your mother? Do you think all this makes Mum proud? Don't just shrug your shoulders, Simon. You need to take a long hard look at yourself.'

Vic was right, as usual. He'd become the moral compass for both our brother, Dave, and me. His words hit their target, hard. There was no doubt about it, my dad's death had floored me. In kickboxing, when you're on the canvas, there are only two options: bounce back onto your feet and fight on, or throw in the towel. I surrendered too easily when Dad passed and I lost my grip on the values he'd drummed into me. The Harley, the Chevy, and the man cave that I was building at the back of our house, were all external masks to disguise the pain inside.

***

THERE'D SEEMED little point in continuing with the kickboxing. Without the incentive of being able to put a smile on my old man's face, it was too tough to work and train at the same time. But I needed something to fill the void. It'd always been hard to watch Fabio and my crew going to pubs and clubs after a training session or a fight, while I dutifully returned home to my wife and baby. But when Dad was diagnosed with cancer I figured that life owed me something. I was ready to cash in that debt and enjoy the new-found attention that I was receiving. As we piled into the pub after my final fight against Brent Porter, I was shocked to find that everyone wanted to buy me a drink, everyone wanted to be my friend. A few girls clearly wanted to be more than friends. One wanted to hold the ice pack to keep the swelling down over my left eye where I'd copped a big hit. Another was keen to rub my back where a couple of decent kicks had found their target.

'What I'd give to be in your shoes for a night,' Fabio said, slapping me on the back.

'What I'd give to be in their pants for a night,' I laughed. It was dawning on me that the itches that had been developing over the years could now be very easily scratched. So, once I stopped fighting, nightclubs filled the vacuum. And I remained the centre of attention, even though I was living off former glories. It was good to drink, to dance, to flirt. I'd missed out on all this. It felt like I'd gone straight from school to being a husband and a father. I'd skipped the fun stuff. Now it was like eating a forbidden fruit. And the more I tasted, the more I wanted. *So what if Vicky's at home holding the baby?* I told myself. *She's only interested in Jake, anyway. I've been slogging my guts out all day, so one more drink's not going to hurt.* I started to creep back into bed later and later and so when Fabio suggested I try my hand at nightclub bouncing, it didn't seem as though my lifestyle would have to change much. As a bonus, I'd be getting paid to keep those long hours. I imagined myself as the Patrick Swayze character in *Road House*, strong-arming the blokes and sweet-talking the women.

***

FABIO LOVED being head of security at the Torquay Hotel, a huge pub down on the Surf Coast. We'd trained together, hunted together and partied together, so Fab knew that he could rely on me. I could spot troublemakers a mile off. When a group of guys approached, I automatically knew who would cause problems and who would act as the peacemaker. The trick was to establish a rapport with the sensible ones, who could help nip trouble in the bud without any need for us to get involved. Sure, some of my colleagues were macho arseholes and too quick to use their fists, but I didn't want any part of that. In no time at all, I was running the show at the Torquay Hotel and my reputation spread. I was soon headhunted by a couple of clubs in Geelong: the Saloon Bar and the Lyric. Often, when I finished my stint in Torquay, I did another shift until 5 a.m. on the way home at one of these clubs. The money was good but the hours were gruelling. It was no life for a young husband and dad. If I came home at six in the morning, Jake would be up and about thirty minutes later, waking me up. So I put a mattress in the man cave and slept there. Vicky and I hardly saw each other and cracks started to appear in our relationship. Time spent together was rare so, when an old school mate who also had a young family invited us all round for lunch one Sunday afternoon, I cancelled my Saturday night shifts so that I could spend some quality time with Vicky and Jake.

'We should do this more often, Vicks,' I told her, slipping my arm around her shoulder as our hosts cleaned up in the kitchen. 'In a few months we won't need the extra money from the bouncing.'

'We don't need extra money now, Simon,' Vicky replied. 'And we certainly don't need any more new parts for the Harley or the Chevy. What we need is for you to be home once in a while. See how different this is when you've had a good night's sleep and you're not cranky? You've really changed over the last couple of years. I want the old you back. I miss him.'

As Jake ran around the garden, laughing and playing with the other kids in the sunshine, and Vicky enjoyed another glass of wine, as relaxed and content as I'd seen her for months, it hit me that this idyllic family life was slipping through my fingers. If I wasn't careful, I might throw it all away. Perhaps this was a good time to quit the bouncing and the late nights, and focus on my wife and kid. Just then, my phone went. It was Fabio.

'Mate, I need a favour, big time,' he said. 'There's a club in Geelong, the Terminus. They need a bouncer tonight and have asked for you by name. It'll be decent coin. Can I tell them you'll be there?'

'Not a chance, Fab,' I said, wandering out of earshot. 'I'm having an afternoon with Vicky and Jake. She will literally chop my balls off if I go to work now.'

'I don't know much about these guys,' he said. 'But I do know you don't want to turn them down. Just show up tonight and tell them it's a one-off. Please. Then I've done my bit and they might not castrate me.' It sounded dodgy as fuck. But Fabio wouldn't have asked me unless he was genuinely worried. Fortunately, Vicky had a soft spot for Fab and when I told her that he was ill, couldn't do his shift at Torquay and might lose his job, she begrudgingly said that I should go. But the optimism she'd built up over the previous few hours was gone for good.

***

THE TERMINUS Hotel was grim – a grey, three-storey, wedge-shaped building made of stuccoed brick on Mercer Street, one of the main roads into Geelong. Two stone steps led up to double wooden doors at the rounded tip of the wedge. The building was probably imposing back in the gold rush days when it was built and it even retained the fancy brickwork on the parapet and above the front doors. There were thick bars over the windows – apparently the place was once a women's prison. A storm was blowing in from the direction of Melbourne's CBD over Port Phillip Bay and, with rain lashing down, the Terminus looked more like a prison again than any kind of club. I decided to park the Chevy a couple of streets away.

I hammered on the front doors for about two minutes and tried to peer in through the windows, which were blacked out on the inside. There was no sign of life and I was about to call Fabio when one of the front doors opened a few inches. A tiny, ferret-like bloke with a big moustache, classic mullet and flannel shirt cautiously poked his head out. 'Yeah?' he said, in that nasally ocker whine.

'Simon Fenech. I was told to be here for six o'clock. I'm doing the doors tonight.'

He pulled the door fully open and ushered me inside, checking behind us that no-one was watching. He placed a long length of rubber pipe next to the door after closing it. Something smelt fishy. And the place really did stink – of beer, ciggies and another sweet scent that I couldn't quite place.

'Denver said you were coming,' he croaked. 'Come highly

recommended. Reckon we might be needing you tonight. There's some serious shit going down. Denver'll tell you all about it. My name's Ferret, by the way. I do the bar. Come and sit inside. Beer?'

'Just a coke,' I replied. 'Don't drink on the job.'

'I'd be having something stronger, if I were you,' he muttered under his breath.

This is a weird club, I thought. *Why's the dance floor raised? Why's the lighting so dim?* The answers arrived in the shape of a tall, slim blonde, carrying my coke on a tray, and wearing a glittery thong, high heels and a cheeky smile. Nothing else. Then the penny dropped. *That explains the pole in the middle of the dancefloor, the blacked-out windows, the smell of cheap perfume.* I chuckled to myself. *How could you be so dumb? Perhaps I'll do a couple of shifts here, after all.*

A steady stream of girls paraded past as I waited for my instructions. Some were turning up for work and entered through a back door, others were putting the finishing touches to their routines and appeared quite happy to give me a sneak preview. And I was happy to watch. Five minutes before the doors were due to open at 6.30 p.m., a bloke in his mid-fifties with that classic bikie look of ponytail and tattoos all around his neck appeared from upstairs.

'I'm Denver,' he said. 'Look, I'll come straight to it. There's a bit of a situation here tonight. If all goes well, we might take you on permanently. Much better than those agency rates you're on. But you may have to earn it. We get some real pieces of work here. One's a fucking psycho called Spinner. Everyone is shit scared of him, and with good reason. He's done time for some serious shit that I won't bore you with. Now he deals speed and makes more money than he knows what to do with. He comes in here flashing it around at the girls like he owns them. They are petrified of him, but he won't take no for an answer and has tried to follow a few home. He's always tooled up, too – knives, guns. Anyway, we tried to ban him last night and he went fucking mental. Told us he'd be back tonight with a sawn-off and is going to take someone out if we don't let him in. There's a chance he won't show, but we can't take that chance. And we don't want the cops sniffing round here for obvious reasons. That's where you come in. We hear you're the best.'

'Even if I am the best, I'm no match for a shotgun,' I said.

'Well, if you can keep him on the other side of those doors, then even Spinner can't cause too many problems.' *Except that I'll be the mug he's aiming at*, I thought. Favour to Fab or not, I was looking for a way out of this when Denver pulled a roll of notes out of his pocket and counted out a grand. 'That's for tonight, with a bit of danger money thrown in. It won't always be that much, mind. Let's just see how it goes.'

At that moment, another of the girls, with breasts that men might lose their minds over, delivered more drinks to the table. 'Skye, this is Simon that we told you about,' Denver said. 'He's the one who's going to be looking after you lot if Spinner shows up.' Skye flashed me a smile that spoke of vulnerability, gratitude and a dangerous sexiness. There was no way I could let these girls down.

Denver gave me a quick tour of the building. The first floor contained private booths, where the girls took punters for an exotic dance. Strictly no touching, just lap dancing. Back at ground level, behind the front doors, was a second set of glass-paned swing doors which opened onto the cloak room, where Denver sat and took the money. These doors were reinforced with horizontal strips of wood below the glass panes, the bullseye for the head of any customer being forcefully encouraged to leave the premises. The rubber pipe that Ferret stuck behind the front doors usually lived beneath Denver's counter, and was three-quarters filled with lead. In the fire cupboard was a sledgehammer handle and, hidden in the ceiling above the bar, a shotgun. Nothing was left to chance. I wasn't sure whether this was comforting, or more evidence that I was in totally over my head. The plan was for me to be stationed in the area between the two sets of doors, where I could keep an eye on what was developing outside . . . but not inside, however much I craned my neck.

Spinner didn't show up that night. Denver pointed out a couple of his associates, including his right-hand man, Jacko. I recognised him immediately. He'd worked with my brother Dave in the trucking business and was known as a wild brawler. His fists, round and gnarled like cabbages, told the story of a hundred punch-ons. Despite the entertainment on offer, his eyes were fixed on me. He'd obviously been sent by Spinner to report on the new security arrangements.

Two weeks passed and still Spinner didn't show. During that time just about the only topic of conversation had been the fucked-up things that he was notorious for. Spinner had worked his way up from being a heavy-for-hire, a standover man, to being one of the most feared men in Geelong's criminal underworld. If you believed everything you heard, he was a torturer, kidnapper and quite probably a murderer. *But he's just one bloke*, I thought. *I'm fit and strong. I'm a champion kickboxer. I fancy my chances against anyone, one-on-one. All the stuff about him is probably just bullshit.* Maybe I was just trying to reassure myself that I was safe.

Then Jacko came back in one afternoon to warn me that Spinner had 'gone off the rails'. 'Who knows what he'll do next,' Jacko said. 'But you seem a decent bloke, so you should know that Spinner never takes a backward step. And he's still spewing about being barred.'

The next day, I turned up for work at 3 p.m. because the club opened all afternoon on a Saturday. Denver wasn't due in for another couple of hours, but Ferret was waiting for me at the front door. 'He's here,' he whispered. I didn't need to ask who. 'Next to the stage with three mates. The girls are shitting themselves but there's been no trouble so far. Should we wait for Denver?'

'Nah,' I said. 'I need to deal with this straight away. Otherwise he's won a battle.' I peered around the door and there was no need for Ferret to point him out. He stuck out like dog's balls, slumped in a chair with his feet on the stage like he owned the place, throwing notes and shouting obscenities at Tigger, one of the more full-figured girls, as she danced the pole. I strode up to the side of the stage and gestured for Ferret to cut the music. Tigger scurried off to the safety of the dressing room. The other punters sensed that trouble was brewing, skulled their drinks and headed for the exit. Spinner's three mates nudged their chairs away from the stage, creating a clear path between us. If it kicked off, I would have to take on all four of them, which I was prepared to do. But I was scared. It would've been stupid not to be.

'Spinner, you know you have to leave,' I said calmly, but with authority.

'Yeah, and who says so?' he replied. I wasn't prepared for the power in his voice, and almost took a backward step in surprise. For such an unimposing frame Spinner had real presence.

'My name's Simon – I'm head of security.'

'Well, Mr Fuckin Simon Head of Fuckin Security, you can go fuck yourself. Put the music back on, bring out a decent bird, and fuck off to your little hidey hole. There's a good boy.' I took two steps forward, as Spinner slowly stood up. We were toe to toe, but I had the height and size advantage. I could also see Ferret in the background, quietly nudging a footstool into position, in case he had to make a grab for the shotgun.

'You know who I am, right?' Spinner asked.

'I do know. But I don't care. You're barred and you need to leave. Look, it's early on a Saturday afternoon. You boys look like you are out for some fun. Just have it somewhere else, okay?'

Spinner let this sink in for a second. 'Well it just so happens, Mr Fuckin Simon Head of Fuckin Security, that we were about to leave this shithole. But just so we're clear, you have made a serious fucking enemy today. I *will* be back.' With that, he grabbed his bottle of beer, kicked over the table, and sauntered slowly towards the door. At the exit, he turned slowly round, theatrically dropped his bottle and left, his hounds trailing behind him, sniggering away.

***

FOUR DAYS later, halfway through a quiet evening shift, Ferret came outside to tell me there was a call for me on the bar phone. 'No idea who it is, but he asked for you by name.'

'Yeah? Who's this?' I asked.

'Remember me, Mr Fuckin Head of Security?' There was no mistaking that ballsy voice, although he sounded different, more manic. I could tell he was off his face.

'Yep, I remember. What do you want?'

'I want you to know, Mr Fuckin Head of Security, that I know where you, your pretty wife and your cute little boy live. Nice part of Hoppers Crossing, isn't it? And I now know that you are at work. And that they are at home alone. So, next time I turn up at the Terminus, I reckon you might want to think about letting me in. Understand?' And he hung up.

My stomach dropped out of my arse. I was seriously rattled, hyperventilating, as I tore out of the club, shouting to Denver that I wouldn't be back that night. It would normally take fifty minutes to drive from Geelong to Hoppers Crossing. That journey took less than twenty. I swerved the Chevy onto the driveway and rushed in to find Vicky curled up in front of the telly.

'You're home early,' she said, sleepily.

'It was dead tonight,' I replied, disguising my panic. 'Is Jake in bed?'

'Er, yeah. Where do you think he'd be at this time?'

Trying not to raise any alarm bells, I dashed to his room, where he was tucked up under his Spider-Man doona. *Thank fuck for that*, I told myself. *But you have to settle this. You can't have a threat from a psycho like Spinner hanging over your family.* There was one obvious solution: quit the Terminus and quit bouncing for good.

43

This was not my battle, and the stakes were way too high. But I couldn't just leave everyone at the Terminus in the lurch, without any back-up. I decided to help them out for one more weekend. That'd give Denver time to find a replacement. I reckoned that if Spinner was going to return, he'd go when it was quiet in the middle of the week and he wouldn't be my problem.

That's where I was wrong. Early on my final Friday evening shift, around 7 p.m., I heard the tell-tale grunt of a Harley pulling up outside. It was Spinner, agitated and menacing, obviously high as a kite. 'Spinner's here!' I yelled to Denver. 'Lock the inside door and the back door, I'll deal with him outside.' Spinner was striding towards the club, both hands in the pockets of his knee-length leather coat. He was known to carry handguns. *This is it,* I thought, *do or die.*

'Fuck off out of here, Spinner. Don't make me tell you twice.' His right hand came out of his pocket, without a gun, and he threw a glancing blow at my jaw. It was nothing. My first punch split his eye socket like a cheap purse. Blood leaked from the gash. 'Leave it at that and fuck off home,' I warned. He staggered towards me, wildly throwing another punch that missed by a couple of feet. He probably couldn't see anything for the blood. I landed another two quick, powerful jabs on his nose. He didn't know what day it was and crumpled onto the pavement. 'Please Spinner, let's not do this. You need a hospital. Stay down, and we'll call you a cab. And then it's finished, okay?'

I shouted for Denver to come to the door, told him to fetch a towel and then to call our friendly taxi service. They were used to picking our leftovers off the street. We heaved Spinner, barely conscious, into the back seat and told the driver that we'd pick up the tab. As the cab pulled away, Spinner wound the window down and, through bubbles of blood, spluttered, 'You two . . . dead.' We knew this was no idle threat and the rest of the night was spent on high alert. Every passing car contained a potential drive-by threat. But, by midnight, there was no sign of him and we hoped the threat had passed.

An hour later, I spotted a white Ford Falcon crawling unusually slowly down Mercer Street. It came to a stop on the opposite side of the road, around two hundred metres away, engine idling. 'Denver, he's here! Clear everyone out through the back and kill the lights!' I shouted, just as the sedan's engine roared and its tyres screeched. Spinner floored it, swerving head on for the front doors. I dived inside and slammed the doors shut a second before the car rammed into the building. It sounded like the club had been hit by lightning. The girls were screaming. The punters stampeded for the back door and the place was empty within seconds, except for Ferret cowering behind the bar and Denver poised for action with the rubber pipe.

Then there was an eerie silence, which lasted for a couple of minutes. *Did he kill himself? Or is he tempting me to come out? There's no chance of that, because he's obviously carrying.* Next came a dull thud on the door, the sound of shoulder against unyielding wood. I could hear him panting and snarling, like a wounded feral beast. Silence again. *Perhaps he's gone round the back. The front's secure enough. I need to check to make sure everyone's cleared off.* As I dashed back through the bar a claw hammer crashed through one of the side windows and landed at my feet. I ducked behind the stage and, through the darkness, could just make out his face, still badly bloodied and now swollen beyond recognition, peering through the broken glass. *Fuck me, he looks just like Jack Nicholson from* The Shining. *Here's Spinner!* I could also see clearly that he was carrying a handgun, which he poked through the broken window.

No way could he see me in the darkness, but I was trapped. And a random shot could have ricocheted anywhere. It was a stalemate. I had no option but to wait for Spinner to make the first move, as he ranted like a madman outside. 'Fucking . . . kill y'all . . . bitches . . . fucking Fenech . . .'

Never has the sound of police sirens been more welcome to my ears. Geelong Police Station was just a couple of hundred metres down the street and a few of the cops were regulars at the club. Someone at the cop shop must have heard the crash and dispatched a squad car. Spinner fled as soon as he heard the sirens but he was quickly tracked down at another pub and arrested. His car remained jammed against our front door. A large, black-handled kitchen knife was found on the front seat, but the pistol was never recovered. Months later, Spinner was charged and convicted of threatening to kill me and Denver, and reckless conduct. While serving time in Port Phillip Prison he was transferred to their psychiatric unit. Perhaps I needed my head examined too for ever setting foot in the Terminus Hotel.

CHAPTER **THREE**

I WAS the man who flogged Spinner, and I wore that label as proudly as any championship belt. In select circles of Geelong's underworld, it carried just as much respect as any kickboxing title.

This was around the time when the hydroponic marijuana scene in Melbourne's west exploded. People were making big money. And where there's big money, there's big crime. The drug trade created the notorious characters of Melbourne's gangland, like Benji Veniamin, Paul Kallipolitis or PK, the Moran half-brothers, Jason and Mark, and Carl Williams – the whole *Underbelly* scene. I would hear these names crop up in conversation at the club, but I was smart enough not to poke my nose in where it wasn't wanted.

I had no idea how much uneasiness there'd been around my arrival at the Terminus. Some thought I had been installed by a rival bikie gang as a mole; others were convinced that I was planted by the cops. Apparently, I was too savvy to be a normal bouncer. It wasn't until the showdown with Spinner that I was accepted and trusted.

Denver – a rough, tough bloke who had a caring side that was completely unexpected – told me of everyone's suspicions. Background checks had been run to make sure that my name and contact details were legit. I was followed and my home was watched to make sure that members of rival gangs weren't visiting me outside of club hours. That's how high the stakes were. During my time at the Terminus, Denver became a mentor – someone I looked up to. He knew how to treat people fairly. If he didn't like you, he'd tell you to fuck off, no messing about. But if you gained his respect, you had a friend for life. He was one of the reasons, along with fearing for the safety of my family, that I stuck around long enough to see off the threat from Spinner.

Another motivation was the girls. They needed protection and, with Spinner out of the way, I was their hero. The girls came from all walks of life – law students, nurses, housewives – and most saw stripping as an easy way to make some good coin and party at the same time. But they all had one thing in common. They were mesmerised by my huge snake.

The boa constrictor was the latest addition to my man cave, which was taking shape nicely. The shed was the size of a single-car garage, with a mezzanine level for my mattress. On the ground floor was a sofa, coffee table, big screen television and my collection of around five hundred die-cast model cars, each in its own perspex case. But the centrepiece was the snake enclosure, a nine-foot-long treated timber box with a glass front and a detachable roof. Inside the box, a thick log ran lengthways, surrounded by fake plants, and a pond in the floor of the enclosure was bordered by gravel. Infra-red lamps kept the enclosure warm.

The boa was only thirty centimetres long and as thin as my little finger when I bought it from a friend of a friend. One frozen mouse was enough to last a week until the snake began to grow – rapidly. It moved on from mice to rats to pigeons and in next to no time the thing was twelve feet long and as thick as my biceps. One of my mates brought a duck round on his way back from hunting. The snake didn't realise it was already dead, crushed it anyway, detached its jaw and gulped the whole thing down. The duck barely made a bulge in its belly.

One day while I was cleaning the enclosure, the bloody thing escaped. I turned the man cave inside out and upside down. Not a sign. I stripped the sheets from my mattress and doona. Nothing. I scoured every blade of grass in the backyard and hunted through every room of the house. Gone. Every night, I checked under Jake's bed and slept with one eye open. Two weeks passed and there wasn't even a scrap of dead skin as a clue to its whereabouts. *Oh well, unless it's a homing snake, that's the end of that,* I thought. *I just hope none of the neighbours have pet rabbits or a Chihuahua.*

On a hot summer evening while driving down to Geelong with the windows of the Chevy down and the 'doof doof' sound of 'Sandstorm' by Darude blaring, a heavy lump of flesh and scales flopped onto my feet from under the dashboard. My instinctive reaction was to kick out and squeal like a pig. The boa, who had been having a nice doze next to the warm engine and wasn't happy at being booted and screamed at, struck out at my ankles. I shat myself, although I knew a boa's bite wasn't poisonous. I veered onto the hard shoulder and leapt out of the car, slamming the door behind me. I was too far away from home to turn back, so I had no option but to take the snake to work. Luckily, an old doona cover that I used for wrapping building materials was in the back of the ute, so I scooped the snake in, tied the top and heaved the writhing package onto the back seat. Passing motorists must have thought I was getting rid of a corpse.

When it'd fallen from the dashboard the snake had become tangled up in the electrics, which were now dangling loose, so I had no headlights or indicators for the rest of the trip. At the Terminus, everyone wanted a look and feel so I wrapped him, now back to his old placid self, around my neck while I stood at the front door. I'm sure we pulled in a lot more punters that night, especially when a couple of the girls volunteered to use him as a prop for their dances. I never looked at that snake the same way again.

***

NOT ALL the girls saw stripping as a fun way to make money. Some were seriously messed up and used me as a shoulder to cry on. Their problems were nearly always down to male influences in their lives. It made my blood boil to hear their accounts of sexual and physical abuse, often from a very young age. One girl in her early twenties, Leanne, told me she had been sexually abused by her uncle. She also told me that she was addicted to heroin but was trying to clean up her act for the sake of her two daughters. She was pretty shocked when I flipped out at the mention of heroin. I despised the stuff. And with good reason.

A few months earlier I'd been delivering a new washing machine to an address in Collingwood in the inner city. I hopped out of the driver's cabin and was about to open up the back of the truck when the morning's tranquillity was pierced by a loud wail. It triggered flashbacks to the trauma of the jet ski accident a few years earlier – it was the same primal wail of a mother in distress. It was coming from a small park down the street and I dropped everything and ran to help. When I rounded the corner, I saw a small graffiti-covered toilet block. The screaming was coming from the ladies and was amplified by the confined space. I ran in and found a young woman with dyed red hair in filthy overalls that hung loosely from her emaciated body. She sat on the toilet and cradled a baby who could not have been more than a few months old. The child's face was purple and her little arm was outstretched as though grasping at something. The baby was clearly dead. Then I spotted the needle, spoon and rubber band on the floor of the cubicle.

'Get the . . . fuck . . . away from . . . me!' the woman screeched, although she could barely form the words or keep her eyes open.

'I'm not going to hurt you,' I said, more calmly than I felt. 'But I need to look at your baby. Honestly, it needs help. Could you just pass her to me?'

'I said . . . keep the fuck away . . . from my baby,' she growled, before slumping down into the confined space between the toilet and the wall, locking the child's body to her chest. 'I didn't kill her. I didn't kill her. I didn't kill her,' she repeated, manically, occasionally breaking off to let out another guttural moan.

I knew what had happened. She'd overdosed and collapsed unconscious onto the baby, suffocating it. I had to act quickly, in case there was any chance that the baby could be resuscitated. Trying to snatch the child would have made things worse, and

I didn't know enough first aid, anyway. I was also wary of grappling with the woman around dirty needles.

My only option was to leave the toilet block and, out of earshot, call an ambulance, then hang around until the paramedics arrived. It was the longest ten minutes of my life. When the ambos finally arrived, I explained the situation, then stood back and prayed. The despondent look on the female ambo's face as she emerged with the tiny limp body in her arms confirmed my worst fears.

After an injection of naltrexone, the reality of the situation hit the mother, who turned feral and started attacking the ambos. I felt like hitting out, too. What kind of person would put her baby's life at risk for the sake of a high? To me, at that moment, the woman had lost the right to be called a human being the second that shit entered her veins. What kind of god would allow that to happen? Not the God I'd been brought up to put my faith in, that's for sure.

I was emotionally shattered and there was no way I could continue with my deliveries, so I headed to the gym to thrash out my anger on the punching bag. When I got home, after telling Vicky in a state of numb disbelief about what had happened, I went to bed. Instead of sleep, the image of that helpless baby's face seared itself into my memory.

There was no way that I could stand by and watch something similar happen to Leanne. So Denver and I called in a few favours to pay for her to go into rehab, on the condition that her kids stayed with a reliable relative while she was away. Leanne was a different person when she returned to work. There was a light in her eyes, where previously there was only fog.

***

WORKING TWO jobs was exhausting, physically and mentally. I barely had enough energy to bounce Jake on my knee, or to grunt a couple of words at Vicky as I headed out the door. It was hopeless. But the solution was obvious – pack in the bouncing. Sure, the money was good but no amount of money was worth putting my loved ones in danger again. And my marriage was in even greater danger. So what was stopping me from quitting? The answer was complex. At the Terminus I was a different man. I was the fella who flogged Spinner. The bouncer with the twelve-foot boa constrictor. I was respected by some very bad men. I was making a difference in the lives of some vulnerable girls, and enjoying a laugh with the others. But rather than admit that I was the problem, I convinced myself that I was married to the wrong woman, was too young to be a dad and was trapped in an uninspiring day job. I used every pathetic excuse available to hide my own shortcomings.

News of Vicky's pregnancy was the wake-up call I needed. This was my chance to turn my back on a lifestyle that was destroying my family. I reduced the bouncing shifts and time at home with Vicky and Jake became precious again. When the adorable Mackenzie was born in March 2004, it signalled a new start on a number of fronts. The franchise owner of Betta Electrical was selling up. It was the perfect opportunity to try something new. My brother, Dave, who was tough, ballsy and streetwise and completely different to Vic, persuaded me to go into business with him. I sold my truck and bought a second-hand Mack Prime Mover. It was every boy's dream to drive a big truck, especially alongside my brother, who I'd looked up to my whole life. It seemed a win-win until the first few months' accounts revealed I was making much less money than before. My solution was to work even harder, often throughout the night, grabbing a kip sitting upright in the truck's cabin. Before long I was back on the treadmill of exhausting hours, and failing to be the husband and father that Vicky craved. Mackenzie worshipped me and wouldn't let me out of her sight whenever I was around, and Jake always showed interest when I was tinkering with the truck or cars. But there was a chasm between me and Vicky. Too much water had flowed under the bridge and the foundations of our marriage had eroded. For me, it was beyond repair.

After a couple of years of sub-contracting for different transport companies with Dave, an old school friend told me of a supermarket with deep pockets that was advertising for drivers. Their distribution depot was only fifteen kilometres from home and they were offering a salary of $130,000 a year, way more than I was making with Dave. It would mean early starts, at around 3 a.m., but I wouldn't have to work through the night. This was another lifeline. Or it could have been, if I hadn't clumsily dropped my application form when handing it in at their administration office. The girl behind the desk bent down to pick up the papers, and I would have gladly worked there for nothing just to see that arse again. My jaw dropped and the girl copped me gawping at her. 'Catching flies?' she laughed.

'Sorry, what an arse. I mean me being clumsy. Not your arse. And not that I'd noticed it. I'll shut up now, shall I?' She giggled flirtatiously.

The job was great, with none of the strapping and tarping

that can chew up half your time in other delivery work. I had a great boss in Lee, a country Tassie boy who I gelled with, and I was chosen to drive a brand-new B-double, around thirty metres in length, with all the latest refrigeration technology. I was also able to invent any number of reasons to drop by the admin office to see if the owner of the arse, Kylie, was around. Not only was she stunning, she had a self-confidence that hooked me in the guts. The fact that I was a meagre driver and she was high up in the admin hierarchy made her all the more enticing. I was soon infatuated.

In her spare time Kylie was a keen showjumper but she'd suffered a terrible accident as a kid when she fell off her horse and was kicked in the face. A brilliant plastic surgeon was flown in from the States and the scars were no longer noticeable beneath her hairline. The accident hadn't put her off horses and, when I found out that she was competing at Werribee one weekend, we arranged to meet up for a drink afterwards. It was a deliberate betrayal of my marriage, because I knew I wanted to start an affair. I'd broken my number one rule – to keep the family together at all costs. But still I tried to justify my actions. The constant internal dialogue drove me crazy.

Look at yourself. What have you done with your life? Fight and work, work and fight. That's all. Do you want to be one of those fat blokes in their fifties, swilling beer on a foreign beach and ignoring their wives? Or do you want to grab another chance at happiness? The kids will understand when they're older. And maybe it's better for Vicky in the long run.

Then Good Simon chimed in.

You selfish prick. Just look at everything you've built. Great home,

great kids and a wife that most blokes would die for. Do you really
want to throw all that away? What has Vicky done to deserve this? It's
not her fault you've grown apart. This is all on you. And you know it's
going to destroy her. Are you really that callous? Where do you go from
here, Simon? When you break your number one rule, you can't fall any
lower. You're not even man enough to tell her what's going on. You're
fucking gutless.

Predictably, Vicky was devastated when I eventually moved
out. She begged me to try to work things out for the sake of
the kids. But my head and my heart were dragging me away.
Packing my bags and walking out the door to stay temporarily
with my brother, Vic, was one of the hardest things I've ever done.
Then, after the initial shock, Vicky found her fury, especially
when she caught me with Kylie at Vic's place while he was away
on holiday.

The empty road is not your friend in times of despair. Travelling
to every corner of Victoria meant hours and hours alone; ample
time for self-recrimination. I was depressed, but didn't seek
help outside of the comfort Kylie could provide. And it was
almost inevitable that my thoughts turned to what seemed like
an easier solution for everyone involved. On a stretch of the
Princes Highway just outside the Gippsland town of Rosedale, a
magnificent, solitary, white ghost gum tree stood at the apex of a
sharp bend, spot-lit by the truck's headlamps. It was like an eerie
signpost to another world that was far removed from the pain I
was causing everyone. So many times I thought above driving
full speed into that tree and ending it all.

***

TIME HEALED. It often does, although I will never fully forgive myself for the hurt I caused Vicky. We were able to reach an amicable settlement, which meant I had to sell most of my toys such as the Harley and the Chevy in order to buy a quarter of the house. I saw a lot of the kids and probably spent more quality time with them than when I was at home. They missed me but seemed to understand why I wasn't around all the time. Kylie and I bought a huge house in Werribee with a spiral staircase and a chandelier in the hallway, three lounges and five bedrooms. We both earnt decent money and were able to pay chunks off the mortgage, as well as treating ourselves to luxuries like a new Harley for me and a beautiful Mercedes coupe for Kylie. The neighbours must have thought that the Beverly Hillbillies had moved in, because this country girl was like a fish out of water in the western suburbs.

In a way, I think Kylie saw me as her little project, upselling me at every opportunity and constantly correcting my grammar. 'There ain't nothing to be ashamed of growing up on a farm,' I told her.

'There *isn't anything* to be ashamed of . . .' she said.

'Yeah, that's what I said. Glad you agree!' To her friends, I was a 'senior heavy vehicle operative', not a truckie. I was happy to play along because, at long last, stability and normality had returned.

***

MY BOSS, Lee, knew that I'd been having a hard time and rewarded my dedication with more responsibility, such as training a new driver called Andrew in a prototype 'smart' B-double, a

660 bhp beast with six spotlights on the cabin roof and all the latest tech like lane sensors.

One of my most frequent trips was to Bairnsdale in East Gippsland, near the New South Wales border, a five-hour drive each way. I felt like the king of the road in this machine and I could tell that Andrew was enjoying the ride. 'Honk the horn,' he laughed when an old Datsun, crammed with presents and a 'Just Married' banner draped across the back window, overtook us. *I hope you two know what you're getting into*, I thought ruefully, then gave them a playful double blast on the air horn.

Just under four hours into the journey the Princes Highway becomes more winding, with big sweeping bends that don't require much braking. On the other side of a small town called Stratford we were approaching one such bend when Andrew sat bolt upright and shouted, 'Brake, Simon! Look at that dust up ahead. Something's happened.'

I slammed on the brakes and shuddered to stop just metres short of two wrecked cars. 'Quick, call triple zero!' I yelled to Andrew as I jumped down from the cab and sprinted towards the first car, which I instantly realised was the old Datsun we'd just seen. Their wedding presents and baggage were strewn everywhere. The driver's door was hanging off its hinges and, sprawled on the road and motionless, was the groom. I checked his pulse but there was nothing I could do for him. The bride was still in the passenger seat, unconscious. Petrol was trickling onto the road and the engine was hissing. It was a recipe for disaster. I went round to the passenger side and tried to force the crumpled door open. It wouldn't budge. I yelled at the woman to wake up. She suddenly snapped back into consciousness, glanced to her right and saw her husband, dead. As she screamed hysterically, I ran back around to the other side and jumped into the driver's seat. The woman was so tightly wedged in that I couldn't even release her seatbelt. Luckily I had a box-cutter, an essential tool of the supermarket delivery trade, in my top pocket. I hacked through the seatbelt and tried to heave her out of the driver's side but her legs were trapped in the twisted bodywork and she was in agony.

'You have to stay awake,' I panted. 'Stay with me. We have to get you out of here. You have to try and pull yourself free.' It was no use. She was in too much pain. I could only hold her hand as a couple of other blokes who had arrived on the scene tried to jimmy her door open with jack levers. In a matter of minutes a helicopter landed in the paddock next to the road and the SES arrived, spraying foam everywhere before using their 'jaws of life' to cut the woman free. An old lady had been helped out of the Ford Focus involved in the collision. It seemed that her airbag had saved her from serious injury. My job was done, but a young SES officer pulled me to one side as the young bride was flown off in the air ambulance. 'Where are you heading now?' she asked.

'I have to deliver this load in Bairnsdale,' I said.

'You shouldn't be driving. You should stay overnight somewhere.'

'Nah, I'm good,' I said.

'Seriously, you should find some counselling when you get home. You've suffered trauma, mate, whether you think so or not. This stuff can really affect you, and for a long time.'

The officer was right. I had nightmares about that poor bloke for a long time. His widow rang me several months later to thank me for my bravery. They'd been married just a few days and were heading home to Gosford in New South Wales after their honeymoon. The nearside wheels of the Datsun had clipped the dirt at the apex of a bend and their car spun 360 degrees and straight into the path of the oncoming car. I couldn't bring myself to ask about her legs. Bones can heal but it was doubtful from the way she spoke so falteringly that this woman would ever fully recover.

I was amazed how detached I had become. It felt like someone else had been involved, not me. Perhaps I was becoming numb to the tragedies that life can throw at you. Were the jet ski death, the heroin addict's baby and this accident part of some mysterious test of faith or character? If so, I reckoned I'd proved myself and it was high time for a break.

CHAPTER **FOUR**

THE DAY that changed my life started like so many others. Jake and Mackenzie had stayed over and I peeped into their room to see them sound asleep before I headed off to work at 3 a.m. Kylie would drop them off at school and Vicky would pick them up in the afternoon. I smeared a burnt slice of toast in butter and Vegemite and shoved the whole piece into my mouth as I hurriedly grabbed the car keys and my backpack. I'd pick up a bacon and egg roll on the way back from my first delivery.

The supermarket depot was mayhem at that time in the morning with perhaps as many as thirty drivers filling their trucks, which were all backed up in a line along the loading bay. The first delivery run was for fresh produce like milk, cheese, veggies and meat. Each driver picked up their pre-loaded pallets using a BT forklift and drove them onto their allocated truck, a single trailer on this particular morning for me. You look a bit like Ben-Hur riding a chariot at the controls of one of these forklifts. But, to see where you are going properly, you have to swivel round and lean outside the cabin. It may not sound glamorous or challenging, but I loved this job. There was a certain satisfaction in the predictable routine of the delivery cycles. I could stop and chat with my fellow drivers, the storemen or the customers at the other end. And I was often home by lunchtime, allowing me to work out, spend time with Kylie, pick up the kids from school on my designated days, and still be in bed at a reasonable hour.

I returned from three drops in Melbourne's east, at Fountain Gate, Beaconsfield and Heidelberg West, and by 7.30 a.m., stomach filled, started to unload my empty pallets ready to fill up again with ambient non-perishable goods, anything from packet rice to toilet paper, for my second run to the northern suburbs. At this time the forklift traffic between the loading bays and the store area was not as busy, because each driver returned from their first run at different times. Three pallets was the permitted maximum and I picked these up with a BT from the back of my truck, drove onto the loading dock and was about to head back towards the stores for the next load.

Another driver, who'd loaded ten empty pallets onto his forklift and couldn't see where he was going, T-boned me from my blind side. It felt like my BT had been hit by a train. I was thrown straight out the open cabin and over the edge of the loading dock, a drop of nearly two metres. I landed on my back and knew immediately that I was in big trouble. My instinct was to try to stand, although I collapsed onto my back again, a lightning strike of agony surging up my spine. Above me I could hear the driver of the forklift screaming for people to come and help. 'Oh fuck, oh fuck, oh fuck!' he yelled, then jumped down to my level. 'Simon, mate, I'm so sorry. I just didn't see you. Where does it hurt? Are your legs broken?' I was struck dumb with shock and was struggling to breathe because the wind had been knocked out of me. I didn't dare move my neck, so my field of view was restricted to the growing number of concerned faces peering over the docking bay. Lee, my boss, and the storeroom manager, Carol, raced over from the control room at the other end of the depot and I managed to mouth the word 'ambulance'. It wasn't until after the ambos fitted a collar and injected me with pethidine, the nerve blocker that's given to women during difficult childbirths, that I dared to even try to wiggle my toes. They barely twitched. *This is not good*, I thought, *not good at all*.

***

FOR THREE hours I lay on a trolley in a packed corridor of the Emergency Department of Werribee Hospital, staring at the halogen lights in the ceiling and wearing just a flimsy paper nightie. As the pethidine wore off, feeling returned slowly to my legs and the pain intensified. Then Kylie was added to the mix. Let's just say she was never one to underplay a drama. We'd only been married a few months, having eloped to Cairns for a private wedding, and hearing about my accident on her way back from dropping the kids at school was too much for her to handle. She was crying buckets before she even spotted me on the trolley. When she saw me, she turned away as though she was going to throw up.

'Hey, I'm still alive,' I said, putting on my bravest face. 'They don't know the damage yet but I don't reckon I'll be on the trampoline tonight.'

'Oh my God, Simon, how can you joke at a time like this? You could be crippled for life. You might never walk again. You won't . . .'

'Whoa, whoa, whoa! Let's try and stay a bit more positive, eh? They're going to keep me under observation overnight but I reckon I'll be home in the morning.' Wishful thinking. An MRI scan revealed fractures of the L5 lumbar vertebra at the base of the spine and the top of the sacrum, the bony structure that connects the spine to the pelvis. Worse still, the fluid-filled disc that acts as a cushion between the vertebra and the sacrum had burst. This meant that bone was grinding on bone and trapping the sciatic nerve. The doctors reckoned that my muscular frame had protected me from even worse injury. Nothing could be done until the swelling subsided, but the pain was so bad I had to stay in hospital under observation for another five days of morphine-induced fog.

I couldn't wait to be back home. But when I was finally released, I soon found that home had become my prison. For three weeks I was a bedridden zombie on the maximum dose of Endone, a heavy-duty and highly addictive painkiller from the same opioid family as morphine and heroin. Add Zoloft, an anti-depressant which also totally numbs your brain, and it was no wonder that I felt barely conscious. I even started watching *Judge Judy*.

And the pain remained unbearable. At first Kylie helped me with everything, including changing my underwear. It was humiliating. Asking for help was not in my nature. People came to me for help, not the other way round. Then, when she had to return to work, I realised just how dependent on her I'd become. The only motivation to leave my bed in the downstairs guest room was to go to the en suite toilet. Bending my back to sit upright was impossible so I first had to lever myself onto my elbows, swivel my legs over the edge of the bed inch by inch, then anchor myself firmly between the armrest of the wheelchair and the edge of the bed so that I could gently lower myself. Climbing out of the chair and onto the dunny was even more challenging and involved grabbing the dunny seat with both hands, hoisting myself up so that I could hold onto the tank, and twisting round until one arse cheek rested on the front of the seat and I could slide back into position. Standing up for a piss was a non-starter. And there was a cruel twist in the tail. A side-effect of Endone is constipation so, when I was finally ready, I had to push hard down through the very part of my back that was permanently on fire. There were times when it was easier to stay sitting on the dunny for a couple of hours, drifting back into uninvited sleep, than go back to bed. The couch was not even an option as the cushions were too soft, making it harder to push myself up again. Showering was only possible with Kylie around although the hospital did provide a Zimmer frame-like contraption which prevented me from falling.

Others in my situation might have asked what they'd done to deserve such agony. I didn't need to ask. The guilt I felt for hurting Vicky was as strong as ever. *This is payback,* I told myself. *Did you honestly think that God was going to let you get away with everything you've done? You brought this on yourself, so suck it up.*

It's not going to last forever, whereas Vicky and the kids may never fully recover.

For a few weeks there was too much swelling around my spine for doctors to properly assess the damage and provide an accurate prognosis. I had to stay patient, battle through this, and focus on my long-term recovery. There were small victories. After a month I could just about sit upright in an armchair, although not for long. I no longer needed the shower frame. I started shuffling between rooms, a little further each day. I made my first sandwich for weeks, although my appetite was poor. I slept for fifteen hours a day, not twenty. Then, at my first out-patient visit to the specialist at the hospital, I was given a cortisone injection into the damaged joint and told that the pain would subside in three or four more weeks. In the meantime I had to attend regular group spinal rehabilitation sessions in St Albans.

Public transport was out of the question and a taxi would have been a waste of money so, despite advice not to drive because of the medication, I manoeuvred myself into the car. Maybe I drove on the correct side of the road, maybe I didn't. The trip was a complete blur. I realised straight away that the group therapy would be a waste of time. The counsellors and therapists wasted so much time breaking down the language barriers with other patients who came from the local immigrant population and barely spoke any English. The program also included sessions in a hydro pool, which is supposed to stimulate blood flow to the injured areas and encourage the body to heal itself. It must have also stimulated urine flow for some people because the pool stank of piss. Each time I was lowered into the pool in a mechanical lift alongside people who looked incontinent through age alone was another blow to my already fragile morale.

For months I persisted with every kind of therapy: physiotherapy, hydrotherapy, occupational therapy, plus an attempt at a bit of sexual healing from Kylie. Not even this, previously the one thing that could be guaranteed to put a spring in my step, could pierce my depression. Another side-effect of Endone is reduced sex drive and, already feeling useless, I was now literally impotent. When my doctor prescribed Viagra the results were startling, but there was a new problem. A side-effect of Zoloft is an inability to come. So I could stay hard until the sun came up, without ever seeing a burst of sunshine. Poor Kylie had arm muscles like Popeye.

Months down the track, progress had been minimal. 'You have two choices, Simon,' the specialist told me at my next appointment. 'You accept that you will always live with a degree of pain, and perhaps never regain full range of movement, or you allow me to operate.'

'Seems pretty straightforward to me,' I said.

'There's a catch. It's a risky operation. The damaged area of your back is the sacral plexus. It's like Flinders Street Station, the main junction for all the nerves from your pelvis and legs. Any one of those nerves could be permanently damaged during the op. There's a chance, for example, that your penis might never work again. How do you feel about taking that risk?'

'How would you feel if I accidently chopped your hands off?' I replied, exasperated. 'You wouldn't be much use as a surgeon, right? Well, I wouldn't be much use as a man. I think I'll take my chances that my back will repair itself, thanks very much.'

A full year after the accident there was precious little sign of recovery. It had taken me all this time to learn my limits. On better days, when the pain was just about bearable, I often tried to do too much, like a walk to the shops, and I'd suffer for the next three days. It was easier to just stay at home, asleep or bored out of my brain. I wore the same trackies all week and changed my T-shirt every three or four days. Normally, I was meticulous about grooming, keeping my goatee neatly trimmed and my head regularly shaved. Now the beard was indistinguishable from the rest of my growth. Pockets of hair sprouted in unruly tufts. There was no limit to the misery and my mental state became as fragile as my spine. My back pain was easy to explain but a disease of the mind like depression was so much more difficult to articulate and understand. Kylie knew I was in trouble but I seemed unable or unwilling to accept her attempts to comfort me.

'It's going to be a slow process, Simon,' she said, 'you just have to grin and bear it.'

'Grin? Did you just say grin? What the fuck do I have to grin about? I look out the window and see grass growing through that load of river pebbles I ordered for the garden the week before the accident. I can't do anything about it. When you go to work and close that door I won't speak to another human being until you come home. I can't stand the kids seeing me like this. It's not fair on them. They don't know how to act around me. A dad should be fun, someone to look up to. Not this shell of a man.

'I don't recognise myself anymore, Kylie. I was so fit and healthy that I used to walk on air. Now I can barely wipe my own arse. I was happy, ambitious. My ambition now? To be able to fuck properly again. It's only a matter of time before you're sick of me. You're a beautiful young woman with your life ahead of you. I'm finished at the age of thirty-two. I wouldn't stick around if I was you. And don't be surprised if I'm not around for too much longer, either.'

'What do you mean by that?'

'There's a lot of pills in this house, you know,' I said, tears of self-pity welling up.

'You can't say stuff like that,' Kylie said, also starting to cry. 'That's not fair. I don't know what more to do to try to help, to show you that I love you. And of course the kids love you, but it must scare them to see you like this. It scares everyone – Vic, Dave, even Vicky. And now you've said that about the pills I'm going to be out of my mind with worry all day. Why don't you see if one of your mates'll drop by?' She stroked my head tenderly. 'Then we can get a takeaway for dinner, okay? That's something to look forward to.' I forced a weak smile, choking back my despair and knowing that I'd take myself off back to bed the minute she pulled out of the drive.

***

FRIENDS DID occasionally visit. It was meant to look spontaneous, but there was probably some kind of rota system involved. I wanted them to stop, because their visits only reminded me of what I was missing out on. Ivon brought an update of how everyone's training was going, because I'd returned to kickboxing before the accident. I was fitter, sharper and smarter, with an aching hunger to reach new heights in a sport that I knew I should've excelled at when I first had the chance. *A year ago he was lining me up for a crack at a world title. Now I couldn't box my way out of a wet paper bag.* Ivon told me of the big things planned for when I returned to training. *Really? Who are you trying to kid?*

Some of my old party mates were on the visitors' rota, often armed with tales of their own relationship troubles, or wanting to relive the events of one of our big nights out. *Not really what I want to hear right now, boys.* My boss, Lee, was a regular, which I appreciated, and he tried to focus on my return to work. *Work? I couldn't deliver a pizza in this state.*

Next it was Bobby's turn, a happy-go-lucky bloke I knew from Werribee. On this particular day my pain was unbearable and I'd closed the blinds so that any visitors would think that I was asleep and leave me alone. When I didn't respond to the doorbell, Bobby just walked around to the back of the house and hammered on the back door. 'Simon, I know you're home, mate!' he shouted. 'Your car's in the drive. Open up, eh? Just want to see how you're going.' I could've just ignored him, because he wasn't that good a mate. My life would have been very different if I had done.

'Okay, okay, I'm coming,' I groaned, hauling myself off the sofa with a wince. 'Oh, Bobby, how's it going, bro?' I said at the back door, trying to sound surprised. 'I was on the toilet.'

Bobby gawped at me like he was staring at a corpse. 'Fuck mate, you look shit. Are you eating properly?' The answer was no – another side-effect of the anti-depressants. I'd probably lost about fifteen kilograms since the accident.

'I eat when I have to. I don't need a lot of energy at the moment.'

'Yeah, I heard you were doing it tough. Look, I've brought you a little pressie. Should make you feel a bit better – and give you the munchies.' He pulled a bag of weed out of his pocket and rolled a joint on the benchtop. 'Scientists are saying this stuff is amazing for pain relief. Reckon it'll be legal everywhere in a few years. If nothing else, it should take the edge off for the rest of the day.'

It was good stuff. Perhaps because I hadn't smoked a joint in a long while, the first drag hit the spot and I felt a warm tingly feeling all over. But the pain was still there, worse in fact. Perhaps the choof had loosened all the muscles which protected the injured disc. Or, being stoned and sluggish, maybe I was focusing on the intensity of the pain. Instead of becoming more relaxed, my anxiety was going through the roof. 'I reckon it might be reacting with my meds, Bobby. Think that's enough for me, thanks anyway.'

'No worries, mate. Maybe I just caught you on a bad day. I'll pop round again in a week or so and you might want to give it another go. Look after yourself, okay?'

I didn't expect to see Bobby again but a week later he turned up and this time the pain was not as bad. It was bearable enough for me to sit upright for half an hour and spend time on the computer. The Aussie dollar was really strong and I was trying to cash in through buying Harley parts from the States on eBay to sell here at a good margin.

'Trying to get me stoned again?' I smiled as I led him through to the lounge.

'Actually, I've got something a bit stronger this time,' he said. 'Have you tried ice before?'

'No mate. It's that crystal meth stuff, right? Some of the strippers were into it at the Terminus but I've heard some bad shit about it. Not for me.'

71

'Look, you need to try something, mate. Reckon this stuff will have you on your feet in no time. It's like speed, but a hundred times better. If it works, just have a bit when you're feeling shit.' On any other day I would have told Bobby to piss off. But I was feeling more adventurous than usual. Or desperate.

'Suppose it can't hurt. But I want to see what it does to you first.'

Bobby pulled a small Ziploc bag out of his jacket pocket and tipped a clear rock, the size of my little fingernail, onto the coffee table. 'You can see why they call it shard, eh? Looks like broken glass.' With a pin that was also in the plastic bag he pricked the rock and it split clean down the middle, revealing distinct layers at the broken edges, like pieces of slate. Out of another pocket he pulled a small glass pipe and a lighter. The bottom of the bowl looked slightly burnt and the inside was covered by a thin white crust. He dropped the shard into the bowl and I was fascinated as he heated it at a slight angle, just enough for the rock to dissolve into a clear liquid and bubbles to form next to the glass. That's when he put the pipe to his lips and, with his thumb and index finger, turned it from side to side so that the hot liquid hit the cooler sides of the bowl, creating an opaque smoke. He never took his eyes off what was happening in that bowl. When there was enough smoke in the pipe, he inhaled deeply, held it down for a couple of seconds and then blew a huge cloud of smoke into my face. It didn't smell like cigarette or bong smoke. It was sweeter and felt almost cool on my skin. It was much lighter, cleaner than ciggie smoke, too. And when it cleared, I could see a huge grin creep across Bobby's face, as his eyes seemed to fix on something from another universe. He poked the pipe in my direction with a grunt, unable to form words to indicate that it was my turn.

'No, not yet,' I said. 'I want to see you go again.' Bobby happily obliged and the effect seemed to intensify.

'There's a bit in the bottom,' he drawled. 'That's enough for your first go.'

'You hold the lighter for me and I'll hold the pipe,' I said, still not sure about the technique. As soon as I saw the stone melt, I sucked it up, but didn't feel a thing.

'There wasn't enough smoke. You forgot to twist the pipe,' Bobby said and grinned. 'It needs to hit the sides.' When I rocked the hot liquid the smoke appeared and I filled my lungs then held my breath for two seconds. And exhaled.

Fuck. Me. One hundred billion nerve cells, from my head to my toes, orgasmed in unison. It was almost too much to handle. My whole body pulsed. *Just. Fucking. Wow.* Every hair stood on end. This high was like an out-of-body experience, a whole different perception of euphoria. Everything was vivid, heightened, beautiful, super-charged. 'Whoa! Fucking hell, man. That is fucking insane. I am flying,' I gasped, when the initial rush subsided after a minute or so. 'I wanna go again.'

'One more piece,' Bobby said and laughed, dropping another shard into the pipe. 'Don't overdo it on your first go. This will keep you going for days.' The second rush wasn't quite as power-ful, but I felt even better afterwards. I suddenly realised that my pain was completely gone. I wanted to hug Bobby. I wanted to hug the whole world. I was alive again – with a vengeance.

CHAPTER **FIVE**

ROOSTER ONE day, feather duster the next. That's how the massive comedown from ice was once described to me, but it took two whole days for me to reach rock bottom after that first incredible high. When Bobby left, I had to clear the thin haze that had settled over the lounge before Kylie got home. I opened all the windows and the fresh air on my face was electrifying. My mind was racing and I had a new, crazy energy. I started a hundred tasks – cleaning the computer keyboard with wet-wipes, polishing the stainless-steel kitchen sink, emptying the fridge so that I could scour the shelves – but finished none. In next to no time I spent another $2200 on motorbike parts on eBay, snapping up anything that looked remotely shiny. It didn't matter whether the parts even fitted my Harley. I answered every ignored text message from the last month. I wanted people to come and see the new me. And I went all out to make an impression on Kylie.

She sniffed the air suspiciously when she walked through the door. 'Have you been cooking?'

'Get used to it, Kyles. I've turned the corner, babe. I'll be cooking every day from now on. Your favourite, spaghetti. Might need a bit more garlic. No more moping about the house . . .' I babbled on, hardly pausing for breath, every gesture exaggerated as though a puppeteer was pulling my strings. '. . . a broken back isn't going to ruin my life. Can never have enough garlic in a spag bol, eh? You're looking at the new me. I'm so sorry for everything. And fresh garlic, not that tinned shit, mind you. No need to worry anymore. How was your day, by the way? Mine was great. I've turned the corner. I'm on it . . .' I was talking so fast that globs of saliva were forming at the sides of my mouth. I was fidgety as fuck.

'I don't know what it is, but I can see you're on *something*,' she said.

There was no point trying to lie. Kylie was too smart. In any case, my pupils were as wide as saucers. 'Look, Bobby brought a bit of that ice stuff round. I had one puff. It's just a bit stronger than speed.'

'It's certainly perked you up. But be careful. I've heard a lot of bad shit about ice.'

I didn't sleep a wink that night. My mind was racing about going back to work, planning a holiday with Kylie and the kids, throwing myself back into training. I watched porn for hours, totally revitalised. Sweating like a racehorse, I cleaned the kitchen, which was a disaster area after my dinner preparations. And I was still at the computer, buying more parts, when Kylie came downstairs in the morning, sulking that I hadn't pointed my new-found vigour in her direction. It'd never entered my head because too much other stuff was buzzing around in there.

I felt good all that morning, with no need for my medications because my back seemed fine. Eventually, around mid-afternoon, exhaustion took hold and I slept on the couch straight through until the following morning. It was a different type of sleep, though. Not the groggy sedation that my medications produced. This was out-cold, dead-to-the-world, fully-clothed unconscious.

Then came the wake-up call. The effects of the meth wore off. The pain in my back, after spending so much time in one position, was the worst since the day of the accident. My head felt like a boulder, heavy and unresponsive. I was back to my most irritable. I had hardly eaten for two days and still had no appetite. But I needed energy and something to wake up my tastebuds, so I forced myself to eat a packet of sour worm lollies that I found in the pantry. The phone continually pinged with messages from everyone I'd contacted after taking the ice. I didn't want to speak to anyone. I took my medications again, because the stupor they produced was more appealing than the way I felt. I was totally sapped of life. Light, natural or artificial, was my enemy and I closed every blind in the house.

I wanted to know why I felt this way so I trawled the internet and learnt that three months' worth of dopamine, the chemical responsible for feelings of pleasure and euphoria, had been dumped into my brain all at once. It would take another three months for my body to fully rebuild those reserves and feel normal again. That's why the second puff didn't replicate the euphoria, just renewed the buzz from noradrenaline, a hormone responsible for increasing heart rate and blood pressure, widening air passages in the lungs, and dilating the pupils – part of the so-called 'fight or flight' response. Meth also fucks with another happy brain chemical, serotonin, and this imbalance can lead to depression, mania or psychosis.

Everything I read told me that ice – or meth, crystal meth, methyl amphetamine, methamphetamine, shard, puff, gear, P, crystal, whatever you want to call it – was probably the most addictive drug on the planet. *Fuck that,* I told myself. *I never want to feel this low again in my life. No more of that shit, no matter how good it is for my back.*

Later that day I heard Bobby's voice at the door, so I hid in the bedroom until he went away. I ignored all his messages saying that he wanted to check on how I was travelling. But after three more days of living hell, I had no option. I had to call him.

'I don't suppose you've got any more of that stuff from the other day, have you?' I asked. 'I'm in bad pain again. It worked well last time.'

'Good stuff, isn't it? Happy to help,' he said and laughed. 'Look, I don't have any on me right now but I can get some pretty easily. But we're flat out at work, and I'm on site at the other side of the city. I'll see what I can do. Do you just want another hundred dollars' worth? We smoked about that amount the other afternoon. I don't mind helping you but listen to me. This shit can take over. And it can get pretty expensive.'

'Don't stress about the cash, I can cover it. I just need a couple of puffs. And don't worry, I've read all about this shit. I know what I'm doing now.'

Four days later, more than a week after that first hit, Bobby showed up. We smoked a point (a tenth of a gram) that morning, before Bobby returned to work. The high was not as intense as the first time but my back pain vanished instantly. I felt indestructible again. When Bobby left, I had another huge puff on my own, perfecting my technique. Soaring all afternoon. Bouncing off the walls. Finally cleared the weeds from the pebbles. Mind sparking like a faulty fuse box. Dinner on the table. Didn't eat a mouthful. Warning from Kylie. Up watching porn all night. Sweats, racing pulse. Slept most of that day. Small puff late-afternoon. Next day bearable. Day after that filthy. Agony, endless tears, darkness. Same the next day. And the next.

It was time to call Bobby again.

***

THE CYCLE of buying a few points and trying to string them out for as long as possible before crashing carried on for a month. Kylie could tell whenever I'd used but I lied about the amounts and made out like it was no big deal. I also tried to schedule the kids to come over when a small quantity of the ice was still in my system. That way I could take them down to the park and happily push them on the swings, something I couldn't have dreamt of doing a few weeks earlier. I even helped them with their homework, confident what I was telling them was correct, even though it wasn't. I was able to start tinkering with my Harley again, fitting the new parts from the States and wondering why the hell all this other shit for Triumphs and Honda Rebels had arrived. I would ease my leg over the seat, start her up and dream about taking her out for a ride again.

When the ice ran out, though, the comedowns became

progressively worse. The drip of a tap would drive me insane. The constant yap of Kylie's babies, five Cavalier King Charles spaniels – Elvis, Britney, Prince, Charles and Camilla – was like machine-gun fire. After pushing my body too far while the pain had been masked, the slightest movement triggered spasms of agony, ten times worse than before. I had to protect myself from this crash scenario. *Doesn't it make sense to smoke one point every day so that the pain never fully returns? A point a day's not going to be a problem. And if I buy in bulk I won't have to rely on Bobby when I'm desperate. I just need to work out how I can afford to smoke $100 worth a day.*

Fortunately, I had a good head for money. I knew there'd be deals to be made. So the next time I called Bobby, I asked how much I'd have to pay for a full gram. Just $700 was the reply. That meant I could smoke a point a day for ten days and only have to pay for seven, saving $300. My WorkCover benefits would cover that.

'You sure you're good with this?' Bobby asked, when I told him my plan. 'I reckon it was less than ten days ago since you bought that last gram. I told you. Don't get fucked up. I know people who have lost their family, home and business to this shit.' He was right. By then I did seem to need a bit more than a point to get me through the day. A gram, which I would split and bag up into points then lock in my desk, was only lasting a week. But the pain had been really bad. I needed just a little extra to cope. *Be strict with your rations and everything will be sweet*, I told myself.

***

MY BOSS, Lee, was a regular visitor throughout the year following my accident. He was genuinely concerned about my welfare and state of mind. He filled me in on the gossip from work and how the business was doing. Before taking ice I didn't want to hear a word of it, but I tried to stay polite. Now, he couldn't shut me up about all the things I wanted to achieve, and all my ideas for efficiencies.

'Jeez, Simon,' he said. 'What a change. I reckon you're just about ready to come back. It's so good to see you back to your old self.'

The reality was that, although my mind was functioning at breakneck pace, my body was still crippled by a broken back. I wouldn't have been able to drag myself up into the cabin of a truck, let alone drive the thing or hook up a trailer. Warehouse work, with all the lifting and twisting, was out of the question. So Lee had no option but to find me other jobs. On the first day back he asked me to arrange some papers in alphabetical order. It took less than twenty minutes and I waited for an hour before my next task, filling staplers. After another hour of watching the clock someone found some filing for me.

'It's worse than doing nothing,' I told Kylie when we met up during our lunch hour. 'It's fucking degrading. I'm way better than this. I'm better off at home.'

'But they'll stop your WorkCover if you turn down the work,' she said. 'And I've noticed there's not much in the bank right now. How much Harley shit have you been buying on eBay, anyway?'

'That's an investment. I'll make money on it. There's no need to worry about money.'

After two or three days of meaningless jobs I was climbing the walls. I picked up a leaflet about health and safety. It was a topic I knew next to nothing about but, after months of obsessing over how my accident could have been avoided, it all clicked into place. I hated reading but I ploughed through anything that contained the WorkSafe logo. *This company's years behind on this stuff*, I thought. *This could be my niche.* I attended the next meeting on occupational health and safety, quickly demonstrated how passionate I'd become about the topic and was soon voted chairman of the committee. I pored over all the workplace incidents and near misses, then worked on new risk assessments. I applied for a part-time diploma and studied during my spare time at the depot and at home.

Working through the night was never a problem, because I was wide awake on ice. I was a conveyor belt of ideas for improvements that might prevent some other poor bastard suffering a similar accident, like safety cages for the forklifts or segregating pedestrians from mobile machinery by introducing designated walkways on the loading dock. Then I tackled fatigue among the drivers and we re-opened a gatehouse to log their hours on the road before allowing them into the compound. If the driver hadn't taken his required breaks, the load would be rejected. The irony was that many of these truckies kept themselves awake by smoking shard.

***

'BOBBY, IT'S Simon again. Tried you yesterday and the day before and left messages both times. I've run out again. What the fuck? Just call me back, okay?' This was not the first time Bobby had gone to ground. I'd always known that his supply would be sporadic. His business always came first. Perhaps I was becoming paranoid, but I also suspected that he might be deliberately avoiding me because he was worried that I was using more than I'd promised.

Or maybe I'd just become a pain in the arse.

My latest order from him had been for half a ball, the equivalent of 1.75 grams, which cost $1000. At the start I would've been paying $1750 for that amount, so I was saving $750 by buying in bulk. By then I was smoking two or three points a day, because the comedowns seemed to be coming around quicker. Running out wasn't worth thinking about. All I could think about was my next puff, that hypnotic twirl of molten shard and mesmerising white cloud. The bigger the cloud, the bigger the buzz. But if Bobby wasn't answering my calls, I needed to find someone who would. That night I stayed up until 3 a.m., too munted to sleep. Through Facebook I tracked down a few of Bobby's friends who I knew were also users. If there was a little green circle next to their Messenger status, they were active, and therefore awake, and therefore using. I sent Friend requests to them all and most responded straight away. I knew one of the blokes from way back.

Hey Ben, remember me?
Yeah, how's it going, mate?
Good. What are you still doing up? LMAO
Can't sleep. LMAO
Me neither. Wonder why! LOL Could do with a bit more to
    take the edge off!!
Might be able to help there ;)
Good man. Any good?
The barra

Sweet. How much?

Sorry bro. Careful what you put on here. Delete that
      comment, eh?

You know where I live, yeah? Can you come to me? I don't
      want to wake the missus by starting the car.

No worries. Give me an hour.

An hour in meth time is like three hours in normal time. It's the worst, because you're all expectant, knowing that an end to the craving and pain is just around the corner. I tried calling Ben a dozen times through Messenger, but there was no answer. And the little green circle had disappeared. He'd probably run out of credit. *He'd better not be fucking me around*, I thought, peering out the curtains every five minutes. At about 5 a.m. I heard a car pull up and park opposite. I saw a bloke in a scruffy tracksuit emerge from the driver's door of a Hyundai Excel Hatch that shouldn't have been on the road. He shuffled across our street and up the drive. I ran to the door to open it quietly, in case he started banging.

'How ya going, Ben? Fuck mate, hardly recognised you,' I whispered.

He looked like the air had been sucked out of his unshaven face. His skin was grey and lifeless, drooping off his skull. The hollows underneath his glassy eyes appeared to be smeared with charcoal. When he opened his mouth to mumble through his remaining teeth, stained and cracked by years of ice use, his breath stank like dog shit.

'Come in, but keep it down, okay?'

And so began a constant procession of vampire-like nocturnal creatures, who snuck through the door of my home in the dead of night. Ben wanted $1100 for the gram, and swore that it was the best stuff around. This was no time to argue over a hundred bucks. I handed him the money and he handed over eight bags.

'Where's the rest?' I asked.

'There's eight points there, mate. I keep two for myself. That's the standard deal.'

I knew I'd just been fucked over but I wanted him out of the house before Kylie stirred. So I pissed him off out the door and disappeared into my room for that mind-blowing first puff. Right there, right then, life was awesome again.

CHAPTER **SIX**

THE HUGE wrought-iron gates outside the house in the western Melbourne suburb of Ardeer were probably worth more than the house itself. We had to circle round the block once just to find a parking spot because the nature strips were crammed with cars, all without number plates, their windows mostly smashed and some jacked up on bricks. There were just as many in the same state inside the gates. The house was patrolled by an edgy bloke wearing shades, saggy jeans and a scruffy jacket two sizes too big. The front windows were partially covered by blankets, not curtains. Rat-gnawed sofas were discarded on either side of the steps leading to the weather-beaten front door, which was guarded by another two intimidating characters. If there had been a neon sign reading *Buy Your Drugs Here*, this ice den could not have been more obvious.

'Are you fucking kidding?' I asked Kurt, a friend of a friend of Ben's and one of the network of vampire user-dealers I'd surrounded myself with. '*That's* where we're buying the gear? This joint looks hot as fuck. The cops could rock up any minute.'

'Relax, this guy's untouchable,' said Kurt, who'd tested my patience once too often.

At first, I had no option but to trust Ben. But soon the bags were marginally less full. Then it started to taste putrid and left too much white dust in the pipe. The hit just about did the job but wasn't as clean as before and the effects wore off more quickly. Ben blamed this on his dealer, who was known to cut batches with MSM, methylsulfonylmethane, a natural dietary supplement used to treat arthritis. It comes in a white crystalline powder but when heated and the sulphurous smoke is blown away it turns into ice-like shards. 'So change the dealer,' I told him. To use another dealer, Ben insisted on half the $1000 up front. I trusted him once and then, second time around, I didn't hear from him again.

'You fucking scumbag,' I growled into his voicemail. 'You'd better hope I never see you around.' Most users would've hunted him down and bashed the money back into existence. I wasn't going to risk going to jail by trying to get blood out of a stone.

Similar things happened with a couple of my other associates. I could normally tell when the ice had been chopped with MSM because the dealer wouldn't want to stick around. It was a different excuse every time: going to do another drop or pick up gear for someone else; going to claim their Centrelink; going to feed the dog. That one was never going to stick because an ice addict would have long since sold their dog. Or, if they suspected that I might suss them out, they dropped a small amount of pure ice into the bottom of their pipe before arriving. What we smoked there and then was very different to the gear they left behind.

86

None of these users had any money, so I was seen as a good customer because I always paid in cash. Their hunger to secure a bit more ice for themselves always took over. Kurt seemed different at first. He was a former tradie who'd been fired because he was always late for work or didn't turn up at all. For a while he didn't try any of the usual tricks, to the point that I was happy for him to borrow my car to pick up the gear. Then he disappeared, with the car and my money, for three full days. I must've tried his phone a hundred times. By the third day, Kylie was no longer buying my story that the car was being serviced. She offered to go collect it, so I had to own up.

'You're using a dealer now? Just how much are you smoking, Simon?'

'Just enough to keep the pain away. And the back's improving every day. It's all under control.'

'Well, you seem to have lost even more weight to me. And you're always tired and grumpy. You sure that's not the ice?'

'Yeah, I'm sure. Now drop it, okay? Kurt will show up. Trust me.'

He did eventually, in the middle of the night, with some bullshit excuse about running out of petrol. But the gear was amazing. For that, I let him off the hook. But there was no way I was going to lend him the car again.

'I'll drive this time,' I told him.

'Nah, man, that's not how it works.' Kurt was smart enough to realise that once I dealt with his dealer directly, I'd have no need for a middleman. But he was hanging, desperate for his next hit, and the lure of three points was too much to turn down. So he directed me to the shithole in Ardeer and told the bloke at the front gates that we were here to see Jimmy D. That was enough to allow us inside, where Kurt was recognised by one of the dealer's foot soldiers. Instinctively, I took off my runners before entering the house.

'Mate, you absolutely don't need to take your shoes off in this joint,' Kurt said and laughed. I saw what he meant. It was a hole. In the first room to the left, two heroin junkies were shooting up on the couch, next to a body on the floor that could easily have been dead. Further down the hall, the first room on the right was stacked with boxes of hot electrical goods like DVD players, power tools, televisions, and a couple of push bikes thrown in for good measure – the currency of ice addiction. In the next room on the left four or five people passed round a bong. I hadn't smoked weed since I began using ice. What was the point?

Back at the front door, a man and woman who were waiting to score were going off at the lookouts. 'When's Jimmy D coming back, mate? We've been here over two hours,' said the woman in a nasally whine.

'He'll get here when he gets here,' came the brusque reply and the pair skulked off. They, like us, had no option but to sit and wait. And wait. This guy was a fuck around. For six hours Kurt and I sat in the kitchen, my anxiety growing with every minute. Not only did I badly want a puff, I was scared shitless that the cops would turn up at any minute. And the conversation with the other customers didn't help my mood. It was all about ice: who had the best gear; who'd been ripped off; who'd been busted, or bashed; whose house had been run through. More often than not the run-through had ended badly, with stabbings or shootings that made the news. *Shit*, I thought. *Word gets around fast. I have a fifty-square house filled with all kinds of valuable stuff. Everyone knows I have cash. I'm sure to be a target if I keep mixing with these people.* I'd never been in a place like this in my life and normally I wouldn't have given these people the time of day. *Make this the last time,* I told myself.

When Jimmy D finally arrived around 2 a.m., there was a scramble to be the first served, but there was plenty to go round. Kurt and I had a smoke in the car outside. It wasn't the pure Asian gear that I'd been promised and had obviously been chopped. That's probably why Jimmy D had taken so long. But seven out of ten was good enough by then.

***

KYLIE WAS right. I was constantly irritable. My body was being punished and my fuse was getting shorter and shorter. Sleep was erratic and the long, late nights were hard to sustain, even with only part-time hours at the supermarket depot. I was using more, too. However good the gear, the highs weren't lasting as long. Within a few months, I was smoking three or four points a day. Bobby was right, too. It was getting expensive. I needed to cut my costs but my back was still too bad for me to reduce the amount I was smoking. The solution was to buy bigger quantities. An eight ball (3.5 grams), which I could get for $1500, would save another grand and might last a couple of weeks. It was a no-brainer.

Now that I was using a middleman less frequently I was able keep my options open. If I knew someone was cutting, then I'd try another contact. These people became my people. This world of deceit, scams and rip-offs became my world. Before, I'd spot a scumbag a mile off. I was intuitive. But the ice had dulled my senses. Like a drunk lurching from pub to pub, I stumbled through the fog, allowing anyone into my inner circle who could steer me in the direction of a quick fix.

On a hot and humid night, I found myself on Barkly Street, the main drag in Footscray, at 3 a.m. in the morning, waiting for some new contact. I'd promised one of the users, whom I knew from previous deals, a point for setting it up but I was about to quit and go home because I'd been there for two hours. I was buzzing from having smoked the last of my stash before leaving so I spent the time fidgeting, cleaning between the car seats, wiping the dashboard and re-arranging the glove compartment. The night was stifling so I got out of the car and waited, polishing the Mercedes badge and wiping squashed bugs from the headlamps. Three Africans approached out of nowhere, laughing and joking.

'Dealer not show, man?' one muttered as they passed the car.

'The fuck you say?' I growled.

'Three in the morning in Footscray, man,' he said. 'No kebab shops open. The wog wants his drugs.' The others burst out laughing. And the red mist descended. I charged at him, smashed the smartarse in the face. His two mates piled on. I managed to land a couple of good punches and was glad to see them all on the ground. Then I felt and heard the flat thud of a brick on the back of my head.

I must have been out cold for a quarter of an hour before I opened my eyes and found myself in the gutter. There was a lump the size of an egg on the back of my head, which was throbbing, and my T-shirt was torn and covered in blood. The Red Bull that

I'd been drinking had spilt all over my jeans. It looked like I'd pissed myself. Bizarrely, one of my shoes was missing. And the money for my drugs, of course, was gone, although the car looked untouched. *There must have been four of the bastards*, I thought. *Or was I set up?*

My mind was still racing when I stumbled through the front door at home, crashing around enough to wake Kylie. 'What the holy fuck, Simon?' she said. 'What's going on? You're scaring me. You need help.'

'Shut the fuck up, will ya? I don't need this shit right now.'

'And I don't need to feel scared in my own home. I found a baseball bat behind the front door yesterday. Expecting anyone in particular?'

I stormed into the downstairs bedroom and slammed the door, unable to cope with another blue.

'Take a look in the mirror, Simon, you're a shadow of the man I married!' Kylie yelled from the hallway. This truth hit a nerve that was already ice-raw. My fist went straight through the plasterboard wall, scraping the skin off my knuckles. Kylie's sobs were lost in the white noise of my scrambled mind.

***

SLEEP OVERCAME me, but when I woke, the atmosphere in the house hadn't improved. My vampire network wouldn't surface for a while, so I was facing a long, anxious afternoon before my next puff. My focus was on getting through those next few hours, not on Kylie's emotions. I decided it was best for me to leave, so I threw some dirty clothes in a backpack and booked myself into an apartment in Flemington. When I eventually located some gear, I'd be able get munted there in peace.

My luck was in and a regular contact agreed to meet me in a nearby shopping centre car park at 5 p.m. It was another hot day. After parking, I dashed into a newsagent to buy a cold drink. Back at the car, my heart sank when I realised I'd locked my keys inside, with my cash for the drugs in the glove compartment. I had no roadside cover – my life was no longer organised enough for that shit – so I asked around the local shops and managed to find a coat hanger and some thin plastic packaging straps. I slid them down the side of the window but couldn't shift the lock. My only option was to call for roadside assistance and join on the spot. Fortunately I had my credit card, which was in my wallet in my back pocket. That was $600 down the drain but I did it anyway. After a couple of hours, a small red-headed guy with a long bushy beard arrived.

'Nothing I can do, mate,' he said, his eyes lighting up when he saw the Mercedes. 'You need a locksmith.'

'So why the fuck did your company just make me sign up? I told them I was locked out.'

'Fuck knows, but I know a good local locksmith. I can give him a call if you like.'

'Yeah, okay. But tell him to get here fast, will ya?'

The mechanic clocked me picking furiously at a sore on my arm, a sure sign of an addict's mounting anxiety. He also noticed the pimples on my face, which were caused by obsessively plucking at hairs with tweezers. He nodded knowingly.

The locksmith, a big bald bastard, arrived within half an hour. He sauntered arrogantly over from his van to speak to the roadside assist man. They looked very cosy and appeared to be laughing at me. *They're saying that I'm getting desperate*, I told myself.

The locksmith slapped his mate on the back and came over to my Mercedes. 'Locked out, eh? I can open it, no worries, but it'll cost you $750.'

'Who the fuck are you trying to kid? Seven-fifty, my arse. Just drill out the lock, you shifty prick.'

'It's now gone up to $900.'

'Are you fucking serious?'

'Nine hundred bucks, mate, take it or leave it.'

I left it, took one step back and knocked him out cold. The roadside assist guy came piling in. He was a tough little fucker and wouldn't go down. It took me ages to sort him out and leave him groaning next to his buddy on the ground. A crowd had gathered to watch the brawl and within minutes four cop cars pulled up. The coppers jumped out, guns drawn. Handcuffed, I was hurled into a divi van. All I could think about was how long it'd be before I could score again. It was almost twenty-four hours since my last smoke and it was months since I'd gone that long without a puff. My head was throbbing and my back pain, aggravated by the fight and the ride in the cramped divi van, was excruciating. It was my first time in a cop shop. Locked in a holding cell while statements were taken from the other two, I curled up in a shuddering ball on the floor.

***

'TWO FIGHTS in twenty-four hours? You used to stop fights, not start them,' said Vic. My older brother was the last person I wanted to see. I'd been charged with two counts of assault and bailed. I was back home. 'You look like shit. No wonder Kylie asked me to come over. What's going on, brother? We're worried about you.' My other brother, Dave, had lagged me in to Vic after turning up at my house one afternoon just as one of the guys who used to deal him speed in his trucking days was scurrying out the door. He knew that nobody used speed anymore, because all the pseudoephedrine was needed to cook ice. Dave was street-smart and realised that if I was associating with this type of bloke, I was already in deep. 'I'll ask you straight,' Vic went on. 'Are you on drugs?'

'I'm on my feet,' I replied with indifference. 'That's enough, isn't it? You should just be thankful for that, eh?'

'Thankful? Thankful to hear that my brother is a drug addict?'

'An addict, eh?' I said, glancing at Kylie. 'Very sneaky. What else have you been telling my brother?' Kylie stayed silent and just stared at the floor.

What followed was almost an exact re-run of the talk Vic gave me at the barbecue all those years ago – beautiful new wife, great home, two great kids, the prospect of returning to a well-paid, steady job. 'Our old man was proud of his son when he died. Make sure that Mum's last memories of you are proud ones.'

Until that point, Vic's words had fallen on deaf ears. I badly needed a puff and had no time for that guilt shit. But mentioning Mum was the one sure way that Vic could penetrate my armour. She couldn't move on after Dad's death and it was hard to watch. Her house remained a shrine to him, with photos on every wall and table, and candles constantly burning in his memory. More often than not she would burst into tears when his name was mentioned. But I loved her dearly and knew that she appreciated my regular visits.

The first warning sign of her failing health came when she served up a tray of pastizzi, burnt to a cinder. A few weeks later she forgot to put them in the oven at all. She was mortified, because the little pastries filled with ricotta cheese were the dish the Maltese take the most pride in. Then, she hopped in her car in the driveway to head to the shops, but stuck the automatic shift in drive instead of reverse and rammed straight through the roller door of the garage. Next, a neighbour told us she'd called around for a cup of coffee. At 3 a.m. in the morning. When we took her to the doctor's, it was no great shock to hear the diagnosis of dementia but we were surprised and ashamed to hear how far it had progressed. Mum couldn't continue to live alone so Vic found her a little cottage within the grounds of a care home where she had access to support and facilities. By the time we sold her house she was unable to even live in the cottage and needed a place within the home itself. She hated it and because Kylie and I had plenty of space, Mum occasionally stayed with us at the weekend for a bit of respite.

'If only I had a daughter,' she complained. 'A good Maltese girl would never abandon her mother like my boys have abandoned me. How can my own son send me back to that place to die alone? How can you do this to me?'

It broke my heart to hear her say those things, so Kylie and I decided that she should come and live with us, despite Vic's warning that the disease was too advanced. But I was determined to follow through on my promise to Dad. Vic was right, though. We couldn't cope. I could barely get through my own day, never mind care for someone who needed constant attention. When Mum messed herself one day I couldn't bring myself to clean her up like I'd cleaned Dad. Although Kylie tried her hardest, we eventually admitted defeat. Thankfully Dave offered to look after Mum at his place, where he lived with his new partner, Carol. He'd had a heart attack, lost his trucking licence and had separated from his wife and kids, but he still wanted to look after Mum. It was admirable.

Mum's illness didn't make me take more ice, but seeing her deteriorate gave me another excuse to detach myself from the real world. I didn't hurt as much when I was high because ice took me to a place where nothing really mattered. It robbed me of the ability to self-regulate, so I was oblivious to the concerns and opinions of others. Vic and Dave had called me an addict to my face. Kylie was convinced, too. I had shut out all my true friends by this stage, and all the people around me used. Strangers on the street, such as the Africans and the mechanics, were taking advantage of my addiction. Yet whenever my mind and body were propelled by ice, I felt in control, indestructible. When the effects wore off, I crumbled straight back into a morose darkness.

The interval between those two extreme states was virtually non-existent – a couple of hours at most – and decreasing with every hit. This was the only time I could cling to the last remnants of normality, before depression washed over me again. During this window I briefly dared to think about weaning myself off. One less point a day would have been a start. My incentive was the prospect of returning to full-time work. Having passed my diploma, which was no mean feat for someone with a dislike of reading and a phobia of computers, I was pretty confident that a new role as a health and safety officer would be created for me.

I was worried about the assault charges and the prospect of going to court. I wasn't sure how my employers would react if they found out. So it was a massive relief when a couple of weeks after the chat with Vic, the charges were dropped. The cops had checked out my accusations that the roadside assist guy and the locksmith were pulling a scam. Sure enough, the mongrels quickly dropped their complaints. With that worry out of the way, I could try to keep my drug use to a minimum in preparation for a return to full-time work. Then, one afternoon as I sat in the gatehouse, tediously counting down the hours before I would be home for another small puff, Kylie rang to tell me that her boss, the regional manager, wanted a chat. *This is it*, I thought, *the game changer.*

'Hello Simon, sit down. How're you doing?' he asked when I got to his office. He spoke again before I had a chance to reply. 'I've been keeping an eye on your rehabilitation since the accident. It's fair to say it's been slow going, hasn't it?' Again, no pause for a response. 'Well, if you remember, we employed you as a transport operator, but I can't see you being back behind a wheel for a long while. And I'm not sure you're even up to a warehouse job. So on that basis we're going to have to terminate your contract and wish you all the best for your recovery.'

'You're sacking me?' I asked, completely floored.

'That's not the term we would use. But leave your keys with Kylie on the way out, please. And, again, on behalf of everyone here, good luck.' The prick stood up and offered his hand. If I'd taken it, I might have pulled him over the desk and bashed him senseless. Instead, I just glared at him, but he wasn't man enough to look me in the eye. My blood was boiling, but I was in shock, too. *What the actual fuck has just happened?* I asked myself. *These dogs cripple me and then sack me? I was a fit, strong, healthy man when I came to work here.* As I left the office Kylie glanced up hopefully from her computer. It was obvious she had no idea what was going on.

'They're a pack of heartless mongrels!' I yelled.

'What? Are you okay?' she asked.

'I'll talk to you tonight, love,' I muttered, barely able to meet her gaze. 'A pack of fucking dogs . . .' I yelled again. Needless to say, I wasn't home when Kylie returned from work.

CHAPTER **SEVEN**

GETTING SACKED was devastating. Any spark of hope for a way out of this mess was snuffed out. I felt like I'd been thrown to the wolves. What hope did a cripple nearing the age of forty have of ever finding work again? There was only one way to escape from the inevitable answer to that question. Smoke more. Up to five points a day, at least. I sank deeper into myself, and found it an ugly place to be. Sleep was a rare relief. Food became an inconvenience. I lost more weight. Not just body fat, muscle too. If my eyes were the window to my soul, then my soul was hollow and lifeless.

Panic set in. Without the security of a regular wage, I wouldn't be able to support my habit and I refused to claim Centrelink benefits. My short-term solution was to buy in bigger quantities. A quarter, or seven grams, would cost me just $2000, another huge saving. But with nothing to occupy my time, it was gone in a couple of weeks, or less. The long-term solution was to start dealing. The intention was never to make money. I was no Walter White from the TV series *Breaking Bad*. Like me, Walter started out as a family man on the straight and narrow. After finding out he had cancer, he realised that cooking crystal meth could provide his family with much-needed security. Greed took over, then evil, although his golden rule was never to touch the product. I wasn't driven by greed and my intentions were never evil. My only motivation to deal was to make sure that I had enough money to cover my habit.

Having been burnt so many times by then, I had to protect myself. So I made people pay me $1500 up front for an eight ball and told them to call back in a couple of hours. In the meantime, I bought a quarter for $2000. My personal eight ball had effectively cost $500. Then I could sell a few points to cover this cost. This meant an even faster turnover of users coming to the house, which drove the wedge between Kylie and me deeper and deeper. We were already living separate lives in the same home. Fortunately for Kylie, she had her precious pooches for comfort. I only had my demons.

Making enough money to support my habit was not a permanent solution to my cash worries, though. After a smoke my mind crackled with ideas. I could still spot a bargain, and I knew my way around cars. Occasionally a good ice deal would mean I had spare cash sitting around, so I put those endless night-time hours to good use by looking for second-hand cars at knockdown prices. I bought a fifteen-year-old VS Holden Calais with more than 300,000 kilometres on the clock for around $1500 off Gumtree. After steam-cleaning the interior, buying some alloy rims and replacing the bumper, I sold it for

$3000. This took me just over a week, and I used that money to buy two more Holdens. The income was crucial, but the work also kept my mind occupied. Unfortunately, good business sense went out the window after a smoke. I started buying anything and everything, even an old school bus from Burleigh Heads up in Queensland for $6500. It made sense at the time – 3 a.m. in the morning! My intention was to convert the bus into a mobile home and sell it to miners in Western Australia who were paying a fortune for their accommodation. The plan was sound but the execution was poor; the bus sat in the driveway for months without being touched. It was soon joined by four or five other vehicles in various states of disrepair. I needed more room, so I stuck them on the nature strip. It was no surprise when one of the neighbours complained to the council and I was told to get rid of the lot.

The answer was to rent a 400-square-metre factory on an industrial estate in Hoppers Crossing. Next to the front roller doors was a glass-fronted area, a bit like a shop window, with an external door that opened onto a reception where I kept the cash register and, later, the Eftpos machine. Behind the reception area was a room which served as kitchen area, tearoom, lounge and office. There was enough space inside and out to store all my vehicles. An old school mate, Steve, joined me to tinker on the cars, happy to be paid in shard. Within five or six months of being sacked I was back on my feet financially. Keeping mobile probably helped strengthen my back, too. It was easier to deal from the factory, away from prying eyes and a distraught wife. Soon I was staying there half the day, then half the night, too. Days and nights merged into one. Occasionally I came home to wash my clothes, grab a tool, or collapse on my bed for a few hours, but I didn't belong there anymore. Whenever our paths crossed, I couldn't stomach Kylie's histrionics, her constant wailing and tears, however well-intentioned they might have been. She somehow believed we still had a future together. I didn't want to hear it and certain phrases burrowed into my skull like termites: 'we can find you professional help'; 'we can beat this together'; 'there's a good man still in there'. But the one that set me off like a firecracker was 'you're a shadow of the man I married'. That truth scythed straight through me.

I wanted out for good and, ironically, was probably closer to Vicky at that point, although she didn't know about my habit. Since I'd started using, I'd tried to shield the kids. It was my one last moral obligation. But keeping a promise is impossible when you're on ice. However clear your objective, the drug has a stronger hold. If I told Vicky to expect me at a certain time, I'd have to defer to what ice told me to do. It's called 'shard time': an extra two, three, maybe even four hours to any agreed meeting. If someone was due to pay me money, I only had one chance to collect. Otherwise that cash would be gone. So that deal became the immediate priority, not my kids. To make amends I showered them with presents like new TVs, or the latest runners, clothes, or video games. 'They don't want presents, Simon,' Vicky said one day when I arrived two hours later than we'd arranged. 'They just want to spend more time with their dad.' But it was becoming impossible to break my work-deal-smoke cycle. I despised myself for it and convinced myself that the kids would be better off without me in their lives. Their mum was loving and dependable, whereas I was a bloody mess. The most effective way to beat myself up was to finally admit to myself that I was a junkie. *A fucking low-life cunt junkie.* But nothing changed.

***

AROUND SIX months after moving into the factory, a windfall landed in my lap. Furious at the way I had been treated by the supermarket, I found a solicitor who agreed to work on a no-win-no-fee basis. We sued the supermarket for compensation for my injury. There was never much doubt that I would win – their lack of compliance with the regulations was obvious. I also had lots of witnesses to confirm that the forklift driver couldn't see where he was going. But I never expected to receive $425,000 ($375,000 after the solicitor's fee was deducted) in an out-of-court settlement. That lump sum could and should have been the ticket out of my living hell. Just think what might have happened had I checked myself into an expensive rehab clinic like Vic, Dave and Kylie were all begging me to do. Of course the money just meant I could buy as much ice as I wanted, so again their pleas fell on deaf ears. The compo payout proved to be the catalyst for a whole new level of shit.

With cash to burn, it was pointless buying anything less than a quarter. I kept enough for myself or whoever was helping out around the factory, and sold the rest on to pay for the next batch. I could also buy more cars. Anything I could lay my hands on, in fact, as long as it wasn't stolen. I bought a 1999 VT Holden Calais, a station wagon, even an HR Holden from the sixties. My stock doubled overnight. Then I found an SS Commodore V8 for $1100 and was about to spend another two grand on it in the hope of selling it for five grand before a random bloke turned up at the factory, specifically looking for V8 engines. He offered me $1500 for the motor alone. I was $400 up before I realised I could sell the transmission separately for another grand and the alloy wheel rims for $800. All up, I sold the parts of that V8 for $6500. It was a lightbulb moment – I was going to open a Holden V8 wrecking yard. Of course the lightbulb was obscured by the smoky haze of five or six guys sitting at the round table in the office. The scene reminded me of the Geneva Convention discussions and so the SS Geneva Wrecking Yard was born, the SS standing for Simon and my mate, Steve, who was still helping out regularly.

Over the next couple of months I bought every V8 that I could lay my hands on and quickly outgrew the space inside and outside the factory. The answer was to lease a vacant paddock about five hundred metres down the road. I bought the best tooling and machinery, racks for the parts, a second-hand forklift and a tilt-tray tow truck. After placing a permanent ad in the Yellow Pages, people from all over Melbourne, from Rosebud on the Mornington Peninsula to the other side of Geelong on the Bellarine Peninsula, even as far away as Wangaratta, rang to sell me their V8s.

I'd stumbled upon a good little business and probably turned over around $80,000 in the first six months. I hoped it would grow to be a legacy for my kids. But I didn't know a spreadsheet from a bedsheet. And the big mistake was mixing real business with drug business. There was no stopping me when I was flying. I made stupid business decisions and the money went straight to my head. Why restrict myself to Holdens? I bought a Chevy Impala for $7500 from Perth but couldn't be bothered to fly there and drive it back, so I just left it there and didn't even chase the money. I bought a classic Ford ute for $28,000 from Townsville and spent another $2800 having it shipped down. The ute that arrived in Hoppers Crossing looked nothing like the picture and was probably worth half the price. So what?

My toys needed replenishing, too. I replaced the Harley that I'd sold when cash was tight, and splashed out on a burnt-orange *Dukes of Hazzard*-style Valiant Charger, confident that I'd make money on them all further down the line. I was burning cash like there was no tomorrow and very quickly half the compo payment had disappeared.

Dave was a regular visitor to the factory and could see where it was all heading. He was at a loose end because Mum was so ill that she'd had to move back into the nursing home. Although VicRoads had reinstated his trucking licence, he couldn't pay to repair his own Mack from an earlier accident. Since a hand-out from me was never an option, I gave him a job driving the tilt-tray truck instead. He was very grateful, but it didn't stop him speaking his mind.

'You need to pull your head in,' he told me, bringing a sludgy instant coffee from the kitchen area to my room upstairs. It was late in the morning and I was sprawled out on the mattress, barely functional after another long night. 'This is fucked, mate. There's too much going on. What happened to your plan to concentrate on V8s? That was a good idea. This way, you're going to run out of money before you know it. People aren't going to come to you for Chevy or Chrysler parts. Everyone around here drives a Holden. And fuck me, Simon, the ice thing is out of control. Look at this place, it's a real junkie's hideaway.'

***

DAVE WAS right, as usual. My ice use had escalated. There were no constraints in my life anymore. I was going through almost two grams a day. That's a point nearly every hour, around $2000 a day at street value but less than $500 at the discounts I was able to find, although I still wasn't dealing direct with the main men. You had to be buying $10,000 worth at a time to have that kind of access. I knew where to buy good gear, though – even if it was only 80 per cent pure, at best. These guys now knew not to sell me heavily cut shit, because I would've just taken my business elsewhere.

Users trusted me. Not only was my gear better than most of the other stuff on the street, they knew where to find me. Sometimes I felt like a prisoner in my own factory, unable to leave in case I missed a deal. I couldn't leave any of the boys in charge as there'd have been nothing left when I came back. Even though I was careful, stuff went missing all the time: wrenches, shifters, demo saws, oxyacetylene torches, jacks or rattle guns. I had little option but to turn a blind eye and replace the tool. These people were doing it much harder than me. I had cash and always knew where my next hit was coming from. So I tried to help out where I could.

One of the young lads who sometimes worked at the factory was locked up for credit card fraud. Identity theft and stealing credit cards from mailboxes was a common way for addicts to make money. Knowing that his wife and kids were doing it tough, I dropped off a few bags of shopping at their front door. I didn't knock. If I'd been seen talking to his missus, word would've reached him in prison that I was visiting for other reasons – a line that could never be crossed.

Another bloke who seemed decent enough took two grand's worth of gear, promising he had a buyer lined up and that he'd make a tidy profit for me. Never saw him again. Anyone else would have taken a baseball bat round to his house and walked out with his TV or anything else of value. But I couldn't punish his family in that way. Imagine the look on his kids' faces. I wasn't callous enough, probably because I knew how much I'd hurt my own family. No matter how many times I was ripped off and cheated I managed to retain my faith in human nature. These were often good people, just in bad places. The disease of addiction caused their darkness, but something good shone through in each and every one of them.

However screwed up I was, it was important that I didn't cross my own moral boundaries. Rule number one was that I never introduced anyone to ice. The people who bought from me were already using and, without me, would've just found another dealer. I never dealt to anyone under the age of twenty, as far as I knew. I didn't accept payment in kind that had obviously come from the family home. Blokes tried to sell me their wife's hair straighteners, their mother's jewellery or their kid's Xbox, just for an extra few points. 'I'm not taking that,' I told them. There was always unskilled work to be done around the factory, like sweeping up, putting parts on the racks, or taking a load down to the tip. 'Come and work for me for a day and I'll pay you in gear. But you have to take your family's stuff back home, bro.' This was also how I responded when anyone that I didn't know or trust asked for gear on tick, though sometimes it was a catch-22 situation. These people usually couldn't work before a puff but then disappeared after half an hour. Rather than chase them down I just felt sorry for them. Another rule was never to sell to anyone who looked too messed up. 'Go home. Sleep it off. Come back when you're not as scattered and we'll talk then,' I told them.

Anyone who brought their pregnant wife or girlfriend for a smoke wouldn't get through the door and was never welcome back. Sometimes, I just didn't like a stranger's shifty expression and told them to fuck off. But it's never easy saying no to an addict. There are always consequences. No doubt I pissed off a lot of people and set myself up for a fall.

Despite my strict code of conduct, and maybe because of it, I had a good name within this huge, hidden sub-culture. I enjoyed being the centre of attention. It reminded me of my kickboxing days. Smoking often turned into a social event. Some men, old school streetwise blokes who'd been around drugs long before the ice explosion, brought their wives for a social puff on a Friday night. I soon learnt that the pipe should never be passed to a woman unless the bloke first gave permission. Truckies dropped by for a puff while their containers were being loaded at the docks. Tradies turned up with a gift of building materials for my new living quarters on the mezzanine floor, such as plasterboard, lengths of timber or a shower tray. This floor, consisting of three bedrooms, one of which had become my upstairs office, a shower room and toilet, plus more storage space, was accessible via two sets of stairs, one leading from the downstairs office and another at the back of the factory. The work was finished in next to no time, at next to no cost.

Other regulars, what I called my 'shoppers', earnt their gear by shoplifting to order. There was nothing these men and women could not steal. One walked out of a supermarket with a trolley full of porterhouse steaks, rib-eyes and Scotch fillets. Another brought me a $600 designer tripod lamp from a hardware store. A pair of Bluetooth speakers? No problem. Lego for Xmas presents? How many boxes? My 'wardrobe' was full of perfectly fitting G-Star jeans. All delivered to my doorstep in exchange for the odd gram here and there.

***

FINDING BLOKES to help scrap the cars was never difficult. The offer of a bit of cash in hand and a puff before work, at lunch and late in the afternoon was enough to attract a constant flow of workers. Most had tradie backgrounds and knew their way around cars. Many also needed a place to crash and I made them welcome. The alternative was to sleep in their cars or on the street. At the factory they woke up to a hot shower and a cooked breakfast of bacon and eggs. At lunch I'd throw a couple of chops on the barbie and in the evening the local pizza joint was on speed dial. While ice suppressed our appetites, our bodies dictated when fuel was essential.

A kind of camaraderie developed at the factory. Everyone knew everybody else's business and it was hard not to think of these blokes and some of the regulars as my new circle of friends.

Tony, another dad in his mid-thirties with a $500-a-week habit, often stopped by for a chat and to bring me a Dare Iced Coffee. Occasionally he brought his nine-year-old son, Cody, who loved to watch the guys cutting up the cars. Any deals were carried out well away from kids. For months Tony was a regular customer and always paid up. I didn't need to know where the money came from. Then one week he said his wages hadn't been paid on time. I agreed to front him the regular amount on tick when he promised to sell most of it and pay me double the following week. A few days later, he told me that his sale had fallen through, but he had another big one lined up that night. So I fronted him another half an eight ball. In total he owed me $1500. But if he was true to his word, I would get my money back and make some on top.

The following week he arrived in floods of tears, an absolute mess. 'I don't know how to tell you this, Simon,' he sobbed. 'My Cody's dead. He was hit by a car outside his school. The ambos tried to save him, but he'd gone by the time they reached the hospital.' I was speechless and could only wrap him in my arms as he broke down, bent double with grief.

'Fuck, mate, I don't know what to say,' I croaked through my own tears. 'I loved that kid. He was a great little fella.'

'He loved you, too.'

'I can't even imagine how you're feeling, Tony.'

'It's all down to this shit. I should've been there waiting for him. And you know what? I couldn't even cry because I was that munted when I got to the hospital. How fucked up is that? I can't even pay for a coffin. That deal fell through again, but I promise you'll get your money back. Just give me some time.'

'Forget the fucking money, Tony. Some things are more important than money, okay? Look, I've got a couple of grand upstairs. Use that for the funeral. No need to pay me back, just let me know the arrangements so that I can come and say a proper goodbye. And take this gear,' I added, handing him a bag containing an eight ball. 'It'll help you through the next few days.'

He broke down again, in an incoherent garble of gratitude, and scurried back to his car. I was a mess for the rest of the day. Two weeks later, I hadn't heard anything about the funeral and he didn't answer my calls. I assumed he was grieving too hard to talk. Perhaps he simply forgot to let me know about the service. Then, after another few weeks had passed, I was driving past a servo in Werribee and spotted Tony leaving the shop. Holding Cody's hand. Happily eating an ice cream. I did a double-take, so stunned that I nearly slammed into the back of the car in front. Definitely Tony, and definitely Cody. I should've been furious. I should've done a U-turn and tracked him down. Instead, sadness overwhelmed me. I'd treated this man how a fellow human being should be treated and couldn't believe that anyone could stoop that low to feed their addiction. From then on, all trust was dead.

***

EVERYONE KNEW that I was dealing. Lots more strangers were turning up without warning. It was only a matter of time before people would try to rob me, as well as con me. The first time it happened, I wasn't prepared. It was a warm night and I'd cleared everyone out of the factory, desperate for some peace and quiet.

I opened the window before finally turning off the lights in my office and stripped down to my boxers. Lying on the mattress, I knew that I'd be lucky if I was able to drift off for a couple of hours. Within half an hour, as I stared at the ceiling dimly lit by distant streetlights, I heard muffled voices. Then a clang, and a grunt. Another bash of metal on metal. It was coming from in front of the factory, where I parked any driveable cars behind the padlocked gates of the main entrance. The area was out of range of the one security camera that had been installed before I moved in. When I peered out of the window I saw three men in hoodies poring over a Holden Torana like hyenas on a wildebeest. They were stripping anything that wasn't welded on. I picked up my baseball bat and crept downstairs, gently unlocking the front door. Two deep breaths and then I charged. The first swing caught one in the arm and he screamed in agony. His mate ran round from the other side of the car and I smashed him on the thigh. He wasn't going anywhere soon. But the third had bolted and was trying to scramble over the fence. When I reached him he was trapped, top half over the other side and his arse and legs forming a perfect target on my side. I managed to land three or four blows before an unwelcome old friend returned – and delivered a sickening thud to the back of my head. The weapon was the Torana's alternator, which I later found covered in blood. I managed to stay conscious, although I was staggering like a drunk after closing time. If they'd wanted to finish me off, one more hit would have done it. Instead, they scarpered as fast as their broken bones would allow.

When the same thing happened two or three more times, but without the fights, I decided to invest in more safety measures.

I installed a $3000 state-of-the-art security system, with around twenty cameras covering every inch of concrete, all linked to a central monitoring system in my office. This was foolproof, as long as I was in the building. But I also needed a deterrent in case anyone tried to break in while I was out. Enter Axel, a gorgeous red-nosed pit bull terrier whom I discovered at the home of someone wanting to sell me a VN Commodore. I could spot a user a mile off and usually secured a better deal after offering them a puff. Through his kitchen window I spotted a tan American pit bull pup, probably not a year old, tied up in the yard with a massive fifty-kilogram chain around his neck. The poor thing could barely stand up under the weight.

'What's with the chain, mate?' I asked after settling the cash and loading the car onto the trailer. 'It's too heavy for the pup.'

'Makes them good and strong, bro.'

'Reckon he'd be better off with me. I'm taking him,' I said, grinning, but more serious than the bloke realised.

'Yeah, righto. He'll take your hand off if you try.' So I tried. And, sure enough, Axel growled as I unlocked the chain. Then he wagged his tail, timidly.

'See, he's going to follow me into the truck,' I said.

'Yeah, righto,' the bloke said again, arrogantly. Sure enough, Axel followed me to the truck. And when I opened the passenger door he jumped up onto the seat.

'See? Reckon he knows he'd be better off with me,' I said, closing the door. The guy stood there, wide-eyed and slack-jawed, as we drove off. Once treated properly, Axel soon became this man's best friend. He greeted everyone with a lick and a furious wag of the tail, but every so often his instinct kicked in and he would bark at a stranger. If that person wanted car parts, I told them I had nothing available. If they wanted drugs, I showed them the door.

With Axel minding the factory, only one weak spot remained: the paddock where I stored the scrap vehicles. It was surrounded by weak cyclone fencing that anyone with bolt cutters could break through. And frequently did – until Black Betty arrived. There was no electricity in the paddock for cameras, so I put an ad on Gumtree for a guard dog. A single mum from Broadmeadows rang and told me that her staffy–pit bull cross was for sale, then brought her to the factory for me to look at. Betty was a pure black chunk of canine muscle but had been beaten by the woman's ex and hated all men. The second the woman drove off, Betty flipped into kill mode and I ran for my life. For two days I was locked out of my own factory as Betty tried to rip through the front door to get at me. My solution was pure genius. From the local sports shop I kitted myself out like a test cricketer: batting pads, gloves, arm guards, a box, of course, even a helmet. Then, armed with a prime cut of beef, I dog-whispered myself into her trust. From then on, she knew that her new owner would never hurt her and she was a pussycat with me. But God help anyone who broke into the yard.

One morning I found her asleep next to a car that was waiting to be stripped. There were fang marks in the door and the roof was clawed to pieces. The windows were covered in her slobber. Black Betty must have trapped a would-be thief in the car for hours before collapsing, thwarted and exhausted. *Bam-ba-Lam*.

CHAPTER **EIGHT**

IT'S ALMOST impossible for friends and family to penetrate the psyche of an addict. Reason is an alien concept, love is from another world, history has no relevance. Contact with my older brother Vic, for so long my life guru, became an inconvenience. He made every effort for as long as possible, with invites for birthdays and Christmas celebrations. At first I showed my face for an hour, but when ice gripped hard, not turning up carried less shame than parading my desperation. He distanced himself from me, and rightly so. He'd tried heart-to-hearts and he'd tried confrontation. There was nothing more he could do.

When he called on the evening of 15 March 2012, my instinct was to flick him through to voicemail. It might be days before I next checked my messages and he could wait. A couple of the lads were finishing up on a car downstairs, so I went down to the factory floor to check on progress. The call was niggling at me, though. Vic and I hadn't spoken much recently. He'd made it clear that his priority was to shield his family from me. Fearing that something might have happened to Mum, I listened to the message.

> *'Simon, it's Vic. Could you call me please as soon as you receive this? Dave's had another heart attack and is being kept at Footscray Hospital overnight. The doctors think he'll be okay. Visiting times have finished for tonight, but perhaps you can go and see him in the morning. He was filling up your tow truck at the big servo on the Princes Highway, so you'll have to go and pick that up tomorrow, too. He was asking for you, so try and get there, eh?'*

Dave's health had been bad for months, ever since the first heart attack, which had also triggered a lot of his money and personal problems. This latest attack wasn't a big shock, but it was alarming nevertheless. After sending Vic a text message saying that I'd be there the following morning, I prepared a quick smoke. Just to take the edge off. Then one of the lads, Jordan, came upstairs for a puff before heading home, leaving me alone with Axel. The evening evaporated. Three hours later Vic called again and this time I answered straight away.

'Dave's dead, Simon. He suffered another heart attack an hour ago. I'll speak to you tomorrow.' He could barely squeeze out the words.

What the fuck? My brother's dead?

I was totally numb. My frazzled brain couldn't cope. Axel climbed onto the sofa, placed his head in my lap and stared up at me with the saddest eyes. He knew I was hurting. For hours I fixated on happy memories of my brother: the knockabout, no-nonsense, salt-of-the-earth guy who would give the shirt off his back for anyone in need. In return, life had crushed him mercilessly.

The next few days passed in a heavy, hideous blur. It's possible that I didn't sleep for more than a few minutes between Vic's call and the funeral. Somehow, I managed to drive to the church in Dave's favourite car, my Ford GT ute. The place was full to bursting. Somehow, I managed to prepare and deliver a eulogy, focusing on his love of trucks. As a kid he often stood for hours on the side of the road just so he could smell the diesel fumes. During one of the hymns, Dave came to me. The vision was so lifelike that I felt as though I could've put my arm around him. He was chuckling away to Mum, happy that I'd promised to look after his pride and joy, the Mack truck, which had consumed his life savings. Mum wasn't even at the funeral; another indication of my frighteningly fragile grip on reality. After self-consciously greeting the other mourners, I slunk away to my cloud of refuge instead of attending the wake.

***

MEANWHILE, BUSINESS was booming. My ice use had also increased and I was up to 2.5 grams a day. It was the only way I could cope with Dave's death. I wanted people around me so I could shut my brother out of my mind. While things were officially over with Kylie, other women had begun to hang around the factory, often friends or sisters of the lads working for me. At this dark time in my life their company was a relief from the same blokes talking the same shit. Michelle was a sparkly, petite brunette in her mid-twenties who wore shorts and skirts that demanded attention. When I first asked for her number, she looked me up and down dismissively, as if to say 'Clean yourself up, first!' Persistence paid off, though, and she began to stay over at the factory every now and then. It wasn't the most romantic of settings, but she seemed happy.

Apart from Michelle, I was wary of allowing women to get too close to my business. It was common knowledge that a lot of the run-throughs and robberies were set up by women, who knew when a home or business owner was likely to be out scoring gear. These women were more vulnerable to being used by cops, too. Many were single mothers with young kids. If a mum was stopped and found to be in possession, it was easy for the cops to persuade them to lag someone in by threatening to have their kids taken into care.

Whether I was snitched on by one of these women or one of the many addicts that I had refused to sell to, I was raided just two weeks after burying my brother. Raids almost always happened first thing in the morning, to try to catch the target off guard. I was alone in the factory but had only been asleep for a few hours when four cars, one marked and the other three unmarked, pulled up to the factory at 7.30 a.m. Axel's barking at the hammering on the front door woke me up and I peered out the window. That type of knocking was not good news.

'Hold on, hold on,' I shouted groggily, as I descended the stairs, buckling up my jeans. When I opened the door Axel couldn't have been happier to greet the six plain clothes detectives and two uniformed officers.

'Are you Simon Fenech?' asked one of the detectives. 'We have a warrant to search these premises.'

'Come in. Can I ask what you're looking for?' There was no point being uncooperative.

'Are there any drugs on the premises?'

'Yeah, there is, upstairs on the coffee table. A couple of grams of ice. For personal use.'

'My colleague here is from the stolen vehicles division. Are there any stolen cars here?'

'Not one. Every car here is legit.'

For three hours they scoured the factory and the paddock. A crowd of interested onlookers gathered from the three adjacent businesses. It was embarrassing, but these guys knew the hours and the company I kept. They knew my game and were probably hoping that I'd be closed down, freeing some of the space that my cars were taking up. At the end of the search the cops told me that I'd be taken to the station to be charged with possession of methamphetamine with intent to supply, possession of stolen goods and possession of unlicensed ammunition. The drugs charge would be hard to defend because of all the paraphernalia in my room. A lot of the workshop tools were obviously hot, but I never asked questions when buying this stuff. So what? I could easily plead innocence on that one. I knew the cops hadn't found a single stolen car part. But the ammunition was a genuine surprise and turned out to be discharged cartridge shells from our farm, which I'd kept in the bottom of some old boxes to refill and reuse at a later date. These guys were thorough. But they were also pissed off that the raid had yielded so little. From the moment I was manhandled into the back of the van until my solicitor arrived at the station and secured my bail, I used my right to remain silent.

The factory was quiet for the next few days. My regulars had heard about the raid and stayed away, as did the lads who worked for me. But it was surprising how quickly everything returned to normal. My customers knew when they were onto a good thing. And I didn't really care about the cops. My life was shit enough already. I wasn't going to be locked up for those offences and it'd be months before my charges reached the courts. Although the workers' compo was dwindling, a few fines wouldn't hurt too much. Perhaps I underestimated the coppers' determination to take me down.

Unbeknown to me, some of the lads were stopping off in the storage compound on the way home and stealing the registration plates off any new arrivals. Hardly any of these guys had valid licences, never mind up-to-date registration on their own cars, so this was a way of buying themselves a few hassle-free months. Fine after fine was clocked up for speeding or running red lights, and occasionally the stolen plates were used to steal petrol from servos. All the notifications were sent to me care of Kylie's address. But she didn't want anything to do with me and didn't pass on my mail. When I was finally tracked down, I'd collected thirty-eight demerit points – twenty-six more than an automatic ban. My excuses fell on deaf ears and my licence was disqualified.

It was impossible for me to run a wrecking yard without being able to drive. Also, I needed to drive to pick up my gear, so I ignored the ban and constantly switched from car to car. This worked most of the time and, before the raid, even though I was stopped on two occasions, I was let off with a slap on the wrist

BREAKING GOOD

and told to leave the car at the side of the road and catch a taxi home. The paperwork wasn't worth the effort. After the raid it was a different story. The next time I was stopped, just a couple of weeks later, I was thrown in the back of the patrol car and charged down at the station. A few weeks after that, the exact same thing happened. I was obviously being watched.

It was no big surprise when the cops turned up at the factory again, two months after their first raid but this time late in the afternoon. Disappointed with their first haul, they probably hoped to catch me in the act of chopping stolen cars. Again, they caught us on a quiet day when nobody was around. The same team arrived and the procedure was rehearsed and very civil. The lead detective even knew Axel by name. After another meticulous search the coppers' reward was a gram and a half, barely enough to charge me with possession again.

'We know you're dealing big time,' the detective said. 'And we know you're running a chop shop. We'll catch you at it soon enough.'

'You're very welcome to come back,' I said. 'But do yourselves a favour next time. Give me a call in advance and I'll put the kettle on. Chop shop, my fucking arse.'

***

SOMEONE CLEARLY had it in for me. It could've been any one of the hangers-on, regular customers or even one of my workers. But if the snitch was telling the cops that I was handling stolen cars, then he or she didn't know me very well. And the quantities of ice that I was dealing were small in comparison to the big players, so they had that info wrong, too. Unable to trust anyone, my paranoia ran riot. My head was spinning. Ice was my safe haven and I needed a near-constant supply just to hold my shit together. One of the blokes who worked for me, Gav, a former bricklayer, told me that word was out that a couple of the local heavyweight gangsters were planning a run-through. I knew their names from the endless chit-chat within our community. These fellas were hardcore scumbags. If an addict ever made the mistake of owing them money, then bones would be broken or skin would be sliced. But dealing wasn't their only vice. Whenever they got wind that someone was holding a big stash, or had lots of cash on their premises, these skunks would turn up, tooled up, knowing that no dealer was ever going to dob them into the cops. I knew from dealing with similar characters during my bouncing days that any sign of weakness would be disastrous. I needed to send a message to them – and anyone else who fancied a pop at me – that I wasn't taking any shit.

It was easy to buy a gun. My associates had these contacts at their fingertips. I was used to handling shotguns from hunting, so this was the obvious choice. A pistol would've seemed puny. A $1200 sawn-off, double-barrelled, under-and-over Beretta made a statement. Work on the living quarters of the mezzanine area had only just finished and, as usual, the plumber had pissed off before finishing the job properly. The tiled wall of the shower ended eight inches below the ceiling and there was a similar gap to the outer brick wall – leaving just enough space to house a shotgun. I fixed a screw on the inside of the shower wall, slipped the shotgun into the gap and hung the strap on the screw. It was perfectly concealed, in the unlikely event that the cops raided me again, and easily accessible if the threats of a run-through came true. The plan was to drip-feed the fact that I was armed to a few people, knowing that word would soon reach the right ears and act as a deterrent. Initially I wasn't going to tell anyone where the gun was hidden. Then I wondered whether it might be worth letting a couple of the lads know, just in case I was in a tight spot and needed help. In any case, the ice took over one night and I blabbed about the gun to too many people. No big deal. With security cameras on every corner, two guard dogs on constant patrol and a shotgun ready and loaded, I felt invincible.

CHAPTER **NINE**

DESPITE ALL the chaos, I made a point of visiting Mum once a week. Watching this once proud woman degenerate made my mood even worse. Often she didn't know who I was – and I couldn't really blame her. I'd begun to avoid mirrors because I didn't recognise the ghost staring back at me. One afternoon Mum screamed for me to leave and complained to the nurse that her neighbour's son had come from Malta to take her away. Soon after, she mistook Vic for my dad and me for Dave, unaware that her second son was no longer alive. Although the doctors had advised us that telling her about Dave's death might cause her to deteriorate even more rapidly, it was hard to imagine her quality of life getting any worse. The decision to keep her in the dark tormented me like an open sore and added to my growing mountain of guilt.

Things got even worse when I took a call from Vic. Almost six months to the day since we'd buried our brother, Mum died.

I dropped the phone and could hear Vic at the other end of the line.

'Sime? Sime? Sime? Are you there? Are you okay?'

I wanted to kick the phone through the window, but I picked it up. 'Yeah, I'm here. Can't believe she's gone.'

'It's just you and me now, brother.'

There was nothing more either of us could say.

When I hung up, my mind went into overdrive, crackling with self-loathing. *So this is how your mother departs this world – unaware that her second son is already dead and that her youngest is a dead man walking. Dad asked me to do one thing – to look after you, Mum. And I couldn't even do that properly. I should've moved heaven and earth to help you out in your time of need. Mum – and Dad – this excuse for a man that I've become is not fit to be called a Fenech, a father or a husband.*

Tear-sodden, I smoked myself into delirium.

***

THREE DAYS later, the day before my mum's funeral, the cops turned up again, mid-morning. This time they meant business. Two new Ford patrol cars, four divi vans and two or three unmarked cars. Four or five of my guys were busy at work and the front roller door was wide open. Someone spotted the cavalcade and shouted upstairs where I was sucking down my second puff of the morning. The lads scattered for no obvious reason. Jordan tried to vault the back fence in one disastrous leap, snagging his jeans and landing face first in the dirt. Gav hid on the roof. He was stuck up there for two hours.

During the first couple of raids I'd been nonchalant, cocky

even. This time I was shitting myself. I had more ice on the premises but that wasn't my main worry; if the cops found the shotgun, I'd be looking at a spell inside. Still, I was confident they wouldn't find it. Now that the mezzanine floor was complete, there were plenty of places to hide stuff. I grabbed the bags of drugs, ran along the gangway that faced onto the factory floor and stashed them under a pile of door trims. Gulping deep breaths to try to calm myself, I was coming down the back stairs when the full team, including four detectives in plain clothes, a dozen or so cops in riot gear and two dog-handlers, marched straight in. Locked in the downstairs office, Axel was not happy. *That's me fucked*, I thought. *The sniffer dogs are sure to find the drugs.*

'Back again, eh?' I asked. 'What are you after this time? And where's your fucking warrant?'

'Cut the shit, Simon,' said the lead detective, a new bloke I hadn't seen before. 'Make this easy on yourself. Where are the drugs? Where are the stolen cars? And where are the guns?'

Fuck me, it didn't take long for them to hear about the gun, I thought to myself.

'There's fuck all drugs here,' I said, handing over a couple of empty gram bags containing just a bit of residue. 'And I keep telling you, I don't do stolen cars. As for guns, I've no fucking idea what you're talking about.'

'I'll ask again, nicely, Simon. Where are the guns?'

'And I'll answer again, nicely. There ain't no fucking guns. What do you take me for?'

'Remind me to answer that when we finish the search,' the detective said, then ordered his team to start going over the place with a fine-toothed comb. They examined my phones and computer, and made a note of every single engine and chassis number, as well as all the parts, and all the wrecks in the paddock. The sniffer dogs pulled their owners excitedly around every corner of the factory, probably following Axel's scent because they didn't find the bags of ice. In one corner, a couple of the riot squad officers made a pile of tools: a demo saw, two grinders and a socket set. Obviously this stuff had been identified as stolen. The hardest part was disguising my relief when a female officer came downstairs and told the lead detective that the shower was clear.

'Right, here's the thing, Simon,' said the detective when his team had finished. 'We know there are guns here. And we're not leaving until we find them. It's going to play out a whole lot better in court if you cooperate.'

'There are no guns here.'

'Okay, have it your way.' He pulled out his phone and dialled a number. 'Yep, we're here now . . . Tell me again . . . Yep . . . Yep . . . Understood . . . Leave it with me.' Without another word he went to one of the unmarked cars and grabbed a sledgehammer from the boot. Resting the handle on his shoulder, he walked slowly past me, grinning sadistically, then theatrically climbed the stairs. Two huge crashes followed. A minute later he emerged, triumphantly holding the half-cocked Beretta. 'What's this, then, Simon?'

'A gun.'

'And how did it get behind the shower?'

'No fucking idea.'

Down at the station I was questioned for around six hours, a pointless exercise because the police's snitch was badly informed. The cops had clearly been aware of my dealing for some time but

I'd never used intimidation or violence to chase debts and it was obvious that I wasn't cooking. Up until the point their informant told them that I was dealing in much bigger quantities than I actually was, I'd been way down their list of priorities. However, the vehicle division were sure I was running a chop shop and, despite three failed raids, were finding it hard to accept the truth. The big problem, though, was the gun and the fact that it was loaded. It didn't help that I'd consistently lied about it, either.

By this point it'd been nearly twelve hours since my last smoke and I was climbing the walls. The cops didn't believe that my mum's funeral was only a matter of hours away. Or had they callously timed the raid to catch me at my weakest? All sorts of conspiracy theories rattled around in my head. Who was the snitch? Only a handful of people knew where the gun was hidden, but Chinese whispers soon became deafening roars in the underworld. Just before midnight I was charged with possession of a prohibited weapon, possession of a loaded firearm, possession of methamphetamine (again), and possession of stolen goods worth approximately $30,000. The detectives wanted me off the streets, but my solicitor persuaded the bail justice to release me on the condition that I signed into the cop shop every day.

Back at my cold, empty and ravaged factory, the desolation was overpowering. From under the door trims, I retrieved the last of my supplies. There's no doubt I would have smoked it all by the time I left for the funeral that morning. But I've no recollection of even being at the church service.

My dad was dead, one of my brothers was dead and now my mum was dead. Vic didn't know how to deal with me. Neither did the mother of my children. Surely Jake and Mackenzie were better off without me. My second marriage had failed and my new relationship with Michelle was going the same way – constantly on-off between furious arguments that were often over stupid things, like whose turn it was to get Slurpees from the 7-Eleven. I trusted nobody. Only Axel provided comfort. I was cast off, rudderless and sinking. Drowning seemed like the logical conclusion to my ordeal. It was an option that was never far from my mind.

***

I SHOULD have realised something was up straight away. Black Betty was cowering and whimpering inside her kennel. Normally she jumped all over me and then ran to the forklift, expecting a ride around the yard. Not this time. After coaxing her out I noticed a couple of deep cuts to her head. She could barely stand. Taking her to the vet was out of the question because she would've had their hands off, so I grabbed the first aid kit from the car and cleaned her wounds with Betadine, then went to the butcher's for a huge marrow bone.

When I got back, I gave the factory a good look-over. Something definitely was up. The cyclone fence had been cut down at the bottom of the paddock where I parked the caravan and the limo. I had intended to restore the limo and run a hire service for parties and special occasions. Now it was just somewhere that I could escape to for a smoke on my own and pretend that I was a millionaire. I'd exchanged some ice for the caravan, thinking at one point I'd take the kids for weekends away.

The padlock on the front gate was cut, too. I checked the yard and found that my truck and tri-axle trailer, worth $10,000 and essential for my business, were gone. A VL Turbo Calais and an expensive gearbox from one of the V8s had also been nicked. And the limo and caravan had been broken into. The thieves obviously came prepared to deal with Betty, probably with a baseball bat. They'd been looking for something specific and wouldn't have been satisfied with the car, truck, trailer and a gearbox. They'd be back.

***

SURE ENOUGH, one week later, they *were* back – Red, Stevo and the Eastern European–looking driver in their olive-green Commodore – this time while I was there. Their little visit landed me in Werribee Hospital, sliced to pieces and shot through the leg. I lost almost three litres of blood. Losing two can be fatal. The doctors said the knife wounds were so deep and so close to my spinal cord that there might be permanent nerve damage. It was outside their expertise so, still unconscious and with blood being pumped back into my body, I was transferred to the Alfred Hospital in Prahran. On the operating table, the specialists found that one of the cuts was two millimetres away from severing my spinal cord. Perhaps my metal chain, which had blocked the final slash, saved my life, or at least prevented paralysis. As I regained consciousness late that night, and the events of the day sank in, survival was no blessing.

When I tried to move my head for the first time the next morning I realised that something was not right. The pain was to be expected, but my movement felt restricted, as though someone was pulling down on my ear and tilting my head to one side. The doctors and nurses thought it was a consequence of the wounds to the muscles around the neck. I was told the tightness would correct itself and full flexibility would soon return. But over the next two days there was no improvement. The doctors became worried that some nerve damage may have been missed. Back on the operating table they discovered that the internal stitching was too tight. Their second attempt at aligning my tattoos was better, too!

Frankly, I was glad of a few days in hospital. The alternative – returning to the factory where I felt under siege – was unthinkable. Michelle was a regular bedside visitor and her support was a much-needed crumb of comfort. She suggested that I stay at her flat in Werribee for a while, but I needed a clean break. What about a couple of weeks with her parents in Mildura? We could say that a car door fell on me at work.

The plan was to cut right down on the ice, although I asked Michelle to pick up my stash before she collected me from the hospital. A couple of the lads visited and smuggled some in to tide me over, but hiding the smoke from the nurses wasn't easy. Up in Mildura, I knew that my gear would be far more effective than any of the pain relief medication.

When stories started to trickle back to me about the attack, it was too difficult not to lapse back into four or five points a day. My one reliable worker, Dave, a non-user, told me that after I went after the driver, the other two, Red and Stevo, forced him to hand over the hard drive from the security camera footage. The whole attack was on that tape. Dave always tried to avoid trouble, so he didn't put up a fight, especially after seeing what had just happened to me. Plus he knew Red, which kicked off a heap of conspiracy theories in my mind. *Was Dave in on this? Or Billy, the other hanger-on who was staying at the factory and had only turned up a few days before the break-in?* Dave was then ordered to drive Red and Stevo to the McDonald's in Werribee, the pre-organised meeting point. The driver was already there, waiting in the car park. 'Reckon I got the prick good,' he said, getting out of the Commodore to greet his two accomplices.

'You were supposed to scare him, not kill him, you dickhead!' Stevo shouted. 'The last thing we need right now is more heat from the cops.'

'You saw the bastard,' the driver said. 'He wasn't going to scare easily. Just pay me and fuck off if you're not happy.' This was the wrong way to talk to Stevo, who punched him in the face. He was soon joined by Red in handing out the driver a proper bashing in full view of the customers enjoying their cheeseburgers. Not only did they take the Commodore, leaving the driver sprawled on the floor, they took his gold watch and chain, too.

The trio must have put aside their differences pretty quickly, though, because they were arrested a week later on suspicion of a drive-by shooting at the Werribee Plaza Tavern. The coppers couldn't pin the shooting on them but they were placed on remand for breaching previous bail conditions. This made me nervous. Their attack on me was unfinished business and I still wasn't sure who was pulling their strings.

The last piece of news from Dave was even more worrying. While I was in hospital, I'd asked Jordan to keep an eye on the factory and feed Black Betty. I trusted Jordan. He owed me. About six months earlier, his home had been broken into while his wife,

Jen, and kids were asleep. Jordan was with me at the time, smoking long into the night. It was probably a dealer looking to recover a debt and Jordan's wife's wedding rings and jewellery were stolen. Jen had previously helped me out with a great deal on some spare parts when her friend's business went bust, so I owed her. In any case, she seemed like a kind and genuine woman who deserved better, but continued to hold out futile hope that her husband was going to turn a corner. She was devastated by the theft of her family heirlooms, so I gave Jordan a couple of grand.

A week into our trip to Mildura, just as I was beginning to realise that a peaceful life away from the chaos and shit might actually be possible, Dave called to tell me that more equipment was missing – around $60,000 worth of tools and parts to be precise – including the other tow truck. There was no way I could continue to trade without that gear. It wasn't clear whether Jordan had been actively selling my stuff, or just turning a blind eye while the other boys helped themselves. Either way, he'd let me down and had some explaining to do. My calls to him went unanswered and I was left with no option but to head back to Melbourne to work out what the hell was going on.

I didn't know what to expect when I got back to the factory. I still didn't know if my attackers had been acting independently or had been sent by gangland bosses higher up the food chain. Those blokes didn't take no for an answer. So I had three choices. The first was to hunt the dogs down when they got out of jail and sort it myself. The likely outcome of that course of action was that I'd end up doing serious time. The second option was to tell the police. But I was no lag, and the cops weren't exactly in my corner. The third option was to do nothing and deal with whatever was thrown at me. It was a solution that would've been unthinkable ten years earlier when I was bulletproof. Nobody would've messed with me back then. Now I was worn out, depressed, in a big black hole and shit-scared. I didn't fancy being stabbed or shot again, so I needed some protection. On the way back to Hoppers Crossing I stopped off to buy another gun – a double-barrelled sawn-off, side-by-side Winchester. It was time to send a message.

CHAPTER **TEN**

THE FACTORY was cold and empty, devoid of the carefree noises of a bustling little business. A strange echo when the front door closed told me how much equipment was missing. Axel headed straight for the poorly cleaned patch of my blood on the floor. He was torn between licking it and his memories of the attack, and so he circled it with a nervous whimper. We were both spooked. I needed to flush the flashbacks out of my head. A couple of puffs would do the trick. It'd help me stay alert, too, because word would soon be out that I was back.

I checked on Black Betty. Thankfully, one of the blokes from an adjacent factory had been throwing meat and bones over the fence. None of my boys had hung around. Work was impossible without equipment and they knew it'd be a while before I was able to deal again. Even my suppliers wouldn't want to know. The spectre of violence sends most people scurrying into the shadows. I had a plan but I needed Jordan's help. I sent him a text.

Know u will get this so don't ignore. No dog would do what u have done to a mate. Come to factory Thurs or will hunt you down.

I was confident it would do the trick. He'd realise there was no way I was going to ignore $60,000 worth of missing equipment. And he wouldn't want me to tell his wife what he'd done. He'd turn up, for sure.

Next, I moved all the furniture out of the downstairs office so that only the desk, one couch and a single chair remained. Then I covered the floor with plastic sheeting. It looked like a scene out of *Dexter*, the TV series about a Good Samaritan serial killer who covered his kill rooms in plastic to hide the blood splatter. The intention was to make Jordan think that I'd flipped and was now capable of anything. He was loose-lipped at the best of times and would soon spread the word that I was no longer prepared to take any shit.

The final part of the plan was genius. I had to keep the shotgun handy, in case it was genuinely needed for self-defence. But the cops could've come back at any minute, so the gun had to be hidden. I took the swivel mount off an old TV and screwed the base to the underside of the desk. Then I duct-taped the shotgun to the mount so that I could sit close into the desk with my finger on the trigger and rotate the gun to aim at anyone standing in the room – without them suspecting a thing. I was so fucked off with life that if someone had come at me again, I may well have used it. I no longer cared about the consequences.

***

JORDAN TURNED up, as expected, snivelling and spewing bullshit excuses the second he walked into the office. Then he stopped dead and stared at the plastic sheeting. His face went white. 'What the fuck, Simon?' he said, his voice faltering. 'I'll help you get the stuff back. You know I will.' I didn't say a word. Instead, I sat motionless and stared hard.

'Seriously,' he whined, eyes pinned on the floor. 'You're freaking me out. This isn't you. Give me a chance to make it up to you.' I let the silence dig deep into his guts.

'Maybe you don't know me as well as you think you do,' I said, slowly and deliberately, wanting to sound slightly psychopathic. 'I'm sick of people taking the piss out of Simon Fenech. You'll work off every cent of what you owe me. Thank your wife and kids that I'm giving you that chance. Now fuck off before I change my mind. Just looking at you is making my stomach turn.' He backed out of the room, almost ran out the front door and sped off in his car. News of my transformation from soft touch to hard nut would be all over the western suburbs before nightfall.

Within a few hours of Jordan's visit, although too soon to be as a direct result, a car pulled into the main driveway. Any car that I didn't recognise was being treated as a potential threat and its crawling speed suggested intent. Racing down from the upstairs office, where I was mid-puff, I barely had time to sit down behind the desk before two blokes strode menacingly through the reception area. The first was a sturdy guy in his mid-fifties with a red bushy beard and tattoos obliterating both arms and much of his face. The second was as bald as a pool ball, shifty, slouching with his hands in his hoodie pocket and eyeing the plastic sheeting with a puzzled expression on his face. If these guys were carrying, experience had taught me to watch the hoodie pocket. I shifted my position slightly so that I could place my finger on the shotgun trigger.

'You're Fenech?' the bearded bloke growled.

'Who's asking?' I replied, trying to appear calmer than my recent puff permitted.

'You know my son, Red.' The ginger gene ran in the family. And my blood ran cold.

'Yeah, I know that piece of fucking shit. You've got a nerve showing your face round here.'

'I've also got this,' he said, drawing a pistol from inside his leather jacket with calculated deliberation. My trigger finger twitched. The ice had primed my body for exactly this: fight or flight. And flight was out of the question. If he'd made a sudden movement for the gun, I might've instinctively fired. He tilted his head at an angle and his eyes narrowed. There was an assured arrogance about him. He'd been in this situation many times. Barely three metres separated us. His gun was aimed between my eyes; my shotgun would have taken both their legs off at the knees. My advantage was that I didn't really care if his bullet ended it all, so I was able to stay composed. *Make the first move, motherfucker.*

'I want to see your statement to the coppers, you fucking lag,' he said.

'What statement? There is no statement. I told the coppers that a piece of steel fell on me.'

'Then how come my boy's locked up now?'

'Because he's a thick prick?' His pistol-carrying arm tensed. 'They didn't even take the knife with them,' I carried on. 'And still I didn't lag them in when the cops found it. It's not my fault they fucked up their next job. Not that surprising, either.'

'Where's the videotape, then?'

'What? Your fucking son has the videotape. Have you actually asked him about any of this?' This stumped him. He looked at his mate for back-up. Baldy shrugged his shoulders then asked, 'What's with all the plastic?' The penny had obviously dropped.

'Renovations, mate. In case it gets messy.' It was time to go on the attack with the dad. 'When you do speak to your son, ask him about my trailer, my truck, the VL Turbo and the gearbox. The three fucking amigos stole them from me a few weeks back. I can't work without my truck. It's one thing going after my drugs money, but that's my livelihood. That's a dog act.' Again, he was lost for words. This guy was clearly old school, probably a bikie. Preventing someone from earning a legitimate crust would've violated his code of honour.

'Nobody told me about that. You sure it was them?'

'It was them all right. They were bragging about it after attacking me. I'm the victim here. I didn't owe them money. They had nothing against me. I was robbed, shot and stabbed at my own place of work. You don't look like the type of bloke who'd stand for that. But I didn't lag them in.'

'If my son's been trying to impress that fuckwit Stevo again, then he'll have me to answer to,' he said after a pause. 'But if I find out that you've been feeding me bullshit, know that I'll be back.'

'And know that I'll be ready for you.'

He liked that. Maybe he appreciated someone with the guts to stand up to him. A slight grin emerged from the tobacco-stained depths of his beard and he returned the gun to his jacket pocket.

And then he did something totally unexpected. He leant over the desk to shake my hand.

***

THE TRUCK and trailer mysteriously reappeared outside the factory one morning while I was at Michelle's. News then reached me that Red and Stevo were out on bail. The cops were still pressuring me to tell them exactly what happened on the day of their attack. Knowing that I still had charges hanging over me, Red and Stevo would have been shitting themselves that I could've put them away for a very long time by doing a deal with the cops. Red would have felt humiliated that his dad had intervened and returned the trailer. It was no surprise therefore when he called me, obviously off his face, threatening to go after Michelle if I cooperated. That pushed me over the edge. Women and kids were off limits. I couldn't live like this, continually looking over my shoulder, not knowing when the next gun would be pointed in my face. The law couldn't, or wouldn't, protect me. If I did lag them in, I'd need round-the-clock protection in the jail system if I was sent down when my case eventually came up. So I genuinely didn't care if I came off second best again to Red and his mates. It seemed a more dignified way to go, standing up for myself rather than digging my own grave with drugs.

'You need to show some balls, like your old man,' I said. 'Come and settle this once and for all, you piece of shit. Bring your two mates. Bring a fucking army, for all I care. You know where to find me. Right where you beat my fucking dog. Tonight. At six.'

My planning was meticulous. First, I chained Betty up in the east corner of the yard where she'd be safe, then wedged the gate open. A dirt drive about fifty metres long separated two walls of scrapped cars and led to the limousine at the bottom of the paddock. I placed a chair outside the driver's door, half-filled two glass coke bottles with petrol and stuck a rag in each before hiding them behind the chair. Next, I collected six ninety-litre gas tanks that I'd salvaged from LPG cars over a period of time and lined up three on each side of the drive, two or three metres apart. The nearest was about twenty metres from the limousine. At 5.50 p.m. I sat in the limo and had the biggest puff. I was hard-wired for action. At 5.58 p.m. I opened all the gas valves, ever so slightly, and returned to the chair. A stunt coordinator of a Hollywood blockbuster would've been proud of the rig. When the pricks turned up and drove through the gates and down the track they would see that I wasn't armed. And the gas tanks blended in with the rest of the scrap. When their car reached the first tank I was going to light one of the Molotov cocktails and hurl it at the second tank. The explosion would blow those scumbags to pieces, and hopefully take me with them. To the outside world it would appear like a terrible accident and my family would be protected from the stigma of suicide.

By 7 p.m. the ice was wearing off. The events of the previous few weeks had taken their toll and I was drained. But however much I craved another puff, I was not going to light up. By 8 p.m. I was on my fifth can of Red Bull, struggling to keep my eyes open. By 9 p.m. it was clear nobody was going to show. Maybe they'd been scoping the paddock and saw what was in store. More likely they showed their true colours – yellow to the bone.

***

THE OWNER of the factory had been unhappy with me for some time and news of the attack exhausted his patience. Several of the other businesses on the industrial estate had complained and I'd also missed a few rent payments when business ground to a halt. My lease was terminated and the owner wanted me out of the paddock, too. But I needed somewhere to store my three hundred scrapped vehicles. The stop-gap solution was to move as many as possible from the factory to the paddock. I used the last of the compo money to buy one twenty-foot and one forty-foot container to store the parts. What was the owner going to do? Move the containers himself?

With the help of Jordan and a few other hangers-on I could continue to strip the remaining cars, fill the containers and then hopefully move somewhere to make a fresh start, well away from Hoppers Crossing – breaking the cycle of violence, threats, paranoia and, just possibly, addiction. Without much cash for just about the first time in my life I couldn't buy in bulk. So I couldn't deal as much and had to cut back on my personal use. It made me realise that I'd been wasting most of the gear for so long. When I was high there was no point smoking more, because I couldn't get any higher. Not a molecule of dopamine or serotonin was left in my body. But cutting back meant that I had to deal with those intense downs again. When I went for days without a puff, I could only cope by locking myself away in Michelle's flat. The back pain, now a persistent sciatica rather than the previous acute agony, flared angrily.

The chance to relocate came from an old contact, Country,

who lived in Dromana, a run-down suburb on the Mornington Peninsula, the other side of Port Phillip Bay. He offered me a room in his house, which had a huge backyard that was soon filled with my containers and my toys: the Charger, the Ford ute, a Harley, a redundant trail bike and a jet ski which had not tasted seawater for many a year. I continued to strip my remaining stock in Hoppers Crossing before escaping on my Harley down to Dromana each night. The change in scenery was supposed to bring peace of mind. But I was convinced that I was being watched. In Hoppers Crossing, all kinds of vehicles, from tiny Hyundai hatchbacks to Toyota Tarago vans with blacked-out windows, were parked opposite the factory at all hours of the day and night or slowly and conspicuously circled the wrecking yard. It could have been cops, or someone looking to settle an old score. I was a nervous wreck.

Since Dave's death I had become friendly with his best mate, Bluey, aka the White Gorilla. At six-foot-four, Bluey had a handshake that would make a silverback wince and a voice that registered on the Richter scale. He'd done time for dealing speed and was now becoming a player on the ice scene. But, like Denver at the Terminus, Bluey was a straight-up bloke who would go out of his way to help a mate. Dave wouldn't have called him a friend otherwise. His home in Braybrook, a small suburb next to Sunshine, was a halfway house for any truckie with a habit and it became a useful stop-off point for me to sell small amounts on my way home to Dromana. The white weatherboard was OCD-induced spotlessly clean and home to a unique collection of all-things Native American – tomahawks, headdresses, wooden totem poles.

One night, heading there to drop off a few grams, I was convinced I was being followed. It was easy to find out for sure. When I turned left, the car turned left. When I turned left again, the car followed. And after one more left it was obvious that this driver was either going round in circles or on my tail. On the Harley it was easy to twist the throttle, weave among the traffic, and lose them before reaching Bluey's.

'You're just being paranoid,' he said, laughing, when I told him about the car following me.

'Nah, I'm telling you. It's either those fuckers who attacked me, or the coppers are sniffing around again. I don't want to lead them here.'

'Well, I can easily find out if it's the cops,' Bluey said. 'Leave it with me.'

I was sure his confidence was just bullshit. A week later I was at the yard one afternoon when he called. I really couldn't be arsed picking up any gear for him that night, so I let the phone ring. He tried about four more times that afternoon and a couple of times in the evening. When I'd finished stripping a car, I called him back, not wanting to piss him off.

'Got something for you if you drop by tonight,' he said.

'What is it?' I asked. 'Can we make it another night?'

'Reckon you'll want it straight away.'

Not wanting to turn up empty-handed, I arranged to pick up some gear on the way and, as usual, was kept waiting for two hours, so it was midnight by the time I reached Bluey's. I parked the bike in his driveway and noticed a few blokes having a smoke under the pergola at the side of his house.

'Want you to meet someone,' Bluey said and smiled. 'Jack, over here, mate.' A little pipsqueak of a bloke in his mid-forties, Eastern European looking with thick bushy eyebrows that almost met in the middle, sauntered over.

'Simon, right?' he said. 'Heard all about you. You might be interested in this.' He handed me six sheets of A4 paper, stapled together. 'That's your police file. Tells you everything you need to know about any ongoing investigations. You're not being followed by any coppers, that's for sure.'

'And how would you get your hands on that?' I asked, struggling to work out what was going on.

'Because I'm a copper,' he said.

'Yeah, right!'

'No, he is,' Bluey said. 'Works at Fitzroy. Don't look so worried. Just trust me, okay?'

Jack nodded and smiled smugly.

What the fuck have you just exposed me to, Bluey? I asked myself, stunned. Here I was, a drug dealer with more than enough gear in my backpack for a charge of intent to supply to add to all my other outstanding charges, being introduced to a serving police officer.

'Er, okay. What do I owe you, Jack?' I asked.

'You got some gear? Let's have a puff,' Jack said. 'Just one thing. See the number at the top of each page? That's my badge number. If this is traced back to me, I'm fucked. So read it, then burn it. Okay?'

'Yeah, no worries,' I said, tentatively. Dealing with bent coppers felt like an escalation to a whole new level, way out of my league.

CHAPTER **ELEVEN**

THE COPS knew more about me than I knew about myself. The file contained my height, my weight, a description of my tattoos, probably my inside leg measurement, too. There was a record of when I went to bed, what time I got up, where I went, and all my associates. The details of my charges were listed and there was also a section on every raid and who'd lagged me in. It had mainly been the hangers-on including a few girls who were never around long enough to have their facts straight, or users whom I'd refused to deal to. Snitching to the cops was a way of getting themselves off the hook or getting revenge. The list highlighted the fact that I could trust nobody. I was exhausted from the constant paranoia, from continually looking over my shoulder. I needed a break from everything and everyone around me. And if that meant a break from ice, then I was prepared to face the inevitable pain. Axel would nurse me through it.

There was so much detail in my file that I stuck the sheets of paper under a few socks in a drawer so that I could come back and absorb it properly at a later date. I packed a few clothes, some food for Axel and hooked up the caravan to a 4WD that I'd moved down to Dromana. Mildura had been a great place to recover from the stabbing and I figured it would make a great place for a healing retreat, too. I didn't tell anyone where I was going, not even Michelle. And I took no ice. Imagine the contrast when I parked the caravan on the banks of the Murray River just outside the town centre but far enough away from prying eyes. Axel leapt straight out of the front seat and chased swallows for all of five minutes before he collapsed, exhausted. I pulled out my fishing rod for the first time in many years and flopped into a deckchair. The warm evening sunshine darted through the leaves of the gum trees and played upon the gentle motion of the river. It was hypnotising.

I spent the next three or four days in a trance, allowing the tranquillity to counter the comedown from the drugs. On ice, I would've wanted to blast the kookaburras out of their trees. Now, their early morning cackling was strangely soothing. My phone was on mute and no fish disrupted my regular naps. A diet of baked potatoes, cooked in the campfire, was just fine. The occasional ciggie was my only vice. Axel never left my side. *I could live here. I need this peace.*

'What do you say, mate? You like it up here? Shall we start again?'

His little tail went bananas.

***

IT DIDN'T last long. The calls started coming thick and fast and the first one was from Country. I'd been stupid enough to introduce him to a young bloke who used to work for me at the factory and needed a place to stay after his parents kicked him out. He was living at Country's when I left for Mildura and he broke into my room, looking for drugs or money. Days later he was caught doing burn-outs on the main drag in Dromana, a breach of a previous suspended sentence. He was going down. My police file, which he'd found in my drawer, was his bargaining chip. He also told the cops where to find my drugs and that I had a gun. The cops swarmed all over Country's house and took anything and everything that belonged to me, including all my toys, except for the containers filled with parts.

'Seriously mate, you're in deep shit,' Country said. 'I'd stay up there if I was you.'

Next came a series of calls from a detective from Professional Standards – internal affairs in other words – urging me to turn myself in for my own benefit and safety. *Fuck me, this sounds heavy.* Then Vicky, of all people, left a message saying the cops showed up on her doorstep and questioned her and her new partner at length. 'Simon, we're all worried about you. Where are you? Jake and Mackenzie know something's up and are really frightened. You have to talk to the police.' Next, Kylie called, then Michelle. The cops questioned them both at their homes and even tracked down Michelle's ex-husband, who barely knew me.

Finally, inevitably, Vic left a message. 'Brother, please let some-one know where you are, or at least that you're safe. I've no idea what's going on, but I'm here for you. Come home, Sime, you're scaring us.' The least I could do was to text him that I'd be home soon and that I was safe. But I didn't.

Firstly, I was trying to keep my phone off as much as possible, in case anyone was able to locate me by GPS. Secondly, I wasn't sure I was going back. Going back to what, exactly? Finding that police internal paperwork had obviously opened a real can of worms. But why was everyone talking about my safety? All I knew was that the bent copper, whose full name was Jack Bennett, pulled a few favours to feed his ice habit. But what if he was well connected, like *Underbelly* well connected? These guys would stop at nothing to protect their interests. Was I now a threat to those interests? Even if I turned myself in, the cops couldn't guarantee my safety, inside or outside prison. I was in a hopeless situation, hunted by the law and the lawless.

Within a week my mood had U-turned from faint hope back to total despair. My isolation was a torture once again, not a relief. I craved my pipe. I would probably crave my pipe forever more. What kind of bleak future did that promise? I was an embarrassment to my brother and my children. I trusted no-one. And now I genuinely feared for my life. Was this wretched existence worth enduring? The Winchester was in the caravan, locked underneath one of the seats. It seemed a neat solution, the best thing for everyone.

But then the phone, the fucking incessant phone, pinged with yet another message. It was Vicky again, sending me a picture of Jake and Mackenzie, leaping into a swimming pool together, with the caption: *Please come home, Daddy*. It felt like a year's worth of tears, backed up by ice and the death of my brother and mother, burst through the dam wall. Axel, beautiful Axel, jumped up into my lap and stared plaintively up into my eyes, his head resting on my belly. He knew my hurt. But only the glimmering embers of the campfire and my short-lived peace died that night.

***

I HAD to return to Melbourne, but I needed to unravel more threads of the mystery before I spoke to the cops. I planned to drop the caravan back at the factory in Hoppers Crossing and then talk to Bluey. Betty did cartwheels when I opened the gates, then spotted Axel in the front seat and went jealously ballistic, so I chained both of them up. After unhooking the caravan from the 4WD, I noticed that two guys had cornered old Charlie, a bloke who worked at one of the other factories and had offered to feed Betty while I was away. Both were in jeans and T-shirts, and could have been detectives or Jack Bennett's associates. Or both. The discussion with Charlie certainly seemed intense. He pointed in my direction and I quickly ducked behind some scrap metal without being spotted. On my hands and knees I crawled under an old Ford F100 truck and climbed up into the empty engine bay. It was a tight squeeze, but I was able to wriggle round so that I could see through the grill. The two guys sniffed around the 4WD and entered the unlocked caravan. Axel sensed a threat and was straining to get at them, growling ferociously. The men were wary and split up to look around the yard, one of them passing a couple of metres in front of my nose, his pistol poking out of his hip holster. He was a copper, not a gangster. Eventually they gave up. Moments later I heard a car pull away from the front of the yard, although I stayed in the truck's engine bay for another fifteen minutes just to be on the safe side.

The next priority was to score some ice. My nerves were frayed and I needed a release. One of my regular dealers agreed to come round to the yard. After two weeks without a puff, the high was out of this world. In case those blokes had somehow followed me from Mildura, it made sense to switch cars. I took a white Toyota Corolla which had a couple of months of rego on it. Axel hopped into the front seat and we headed for Bluey's. At the side of the approach road to the industrial estate I saw a silver Ford sedan parked suspiciously, with two men inside. I pulled my baseball cap down over my eyes and avoided their gaze as I drove past. The Ford pulled out behind me and kept a steady distance for about a kilometre. When I overtook another car, the Ford overtook. I swung a hard left and the Ford stayed right behind me. I zig-zagged through traffic on the road between Werribee and Hoppers Crossing, but the Ford was still in my mirrors. Suddenly, a stretch of clear road opened up. The Ford was stuck behind two cars. I gunned it, even if gunning a Toyota Corolla felt more like firing a water pistol. The Ford swerved from side to side, desperately looking for an opening before the two cars pulled over. In the rear-view mirror I could tell that the Ford was gaining quickly. It was no contest, and probably meant that it was an undercover cop car.

But good cops, or bad cops? Why no lights or sirens? I couldn't take a chance and kept my foot on the gas. Out of nowhere a patrol car sped directly towards me on my side of the road with lights flashing and sirens blaring. I swerved onto the nature strip, bouncing Axel off the roof. He thought it was great fun. Up ahead was a major intersection and the lights were red. Feeling bulletproof from the ice, I closed my eyes and hurtled on. Tyres screeched, horns blared, but I made it across. In the rear-view mirror I could see the mayhem that I'd caused at the junction. Two hundred metres ahead was a big roundabout and, approaching at full speed with the intention of ploughing straight through, I spotted two more patrol cars blocking my exit. I veered hard left into the Werribee Plaza car park. Axel landed in my lap and took his chance to join in the fun by licking my face. *Not helpful, mate.* Carefully weaving between shoppers and parked cars I emerged out the other side of the car park and heard the sirens of another cop car close on my tail. The side street was lined with speed chicanes and up ahead yet another patrol car blocked the road, but I convinced myself there was just enough of a gap between the rear bumper and a ghost gum on the footpath. It was the ice talking. The Corolla slammed headfirst into the tree and my head broke the windscreen. My first thought was to run. I scrabbled at my seatbelt, but couldn't see through the blood gushing from my forehead. Within seconds I had help, with several pairs of hands hauling me out of the driver's seat and onto my front on the pavement, cuffing my hands behind my back. Axel was snarling and barking furiously in the back of the Toyota and I heard one cop shout, 'Someone shoot that fucking dog!'

'No, not the dog,' I gurgled, trying to twist around to see what was happening. 'Please don't hurt my dog. Axel, it's okay, mate. Calm down, good boy.'

'Shut the fuck up,' growled one of the coppers on top of me, jamming my cheek into the concrete so that I couldn't even talk. 'There's only one dog we're interested in.'

***

WERRIBEE POLICE Station was hostile, except for one female officer who was furious that an ambulance hadn't been called. The jagged gash on my forehead stretched from the outside of one eyebrow to the other. Only the towel, wrapped tightly around my head, was preventing the wound from flapping open.

'Where's Axel? Is my dog here?' I mumbled, concussed and barely conscious.

The ambos were also disgusted at the way I'd been treated. 'This man should never have been moved!' one shouted. 'He should've been placed in a neck brace at the scene of the accident. Look at that wound. His nose is clearly broken, so why not his neck, too?'

Heavily sedated, I was taken to Werribee Hospital under police guard. When I came round I found myself in a private ward at Footscray Hospital. Two detectives were chatting away at the side of the bed. One wore a long black coat, like someone out of the Gestapo. They were talking about my case, so I pretended to be asleep. Bennett had been arrested. And they'd found nothing at Bluey's. His precious collection of tomahawks and various other knives were seized and I felt rotten that I'd brought this heat on him.

'The dog's with the ranger,' I then heard one of the cops say.

'He'll be put down for sure.'

'What?' I shouted. 'Don't hurt the dog! Please, he's all I've got.'

'Ah, Mr Fenech, you're back with us. I thought that would wake you up. How are you doing? The plastic surgeon's done a great job. No more beauty contests, though. And don't worry, I will find out about the dog.' It turned out both detectives were from Professional Standards, the cops who investigate bad cops. They were worryingly pleasant while I remained under guard in the hospital. Their focus was on Bennett but it was in my interests to stay silent. *Trust no-one*, I told myself.

Bandaged and still groggy, I was transferred to the Victoria Police headquarters on Flinders Street and interrogated non-stop for the next twenty-four hours. No sleep, no solicitor, no ciggies, no dignity. The detectives went on and on about my association with Bennett. How long had I known him? I'd never even heard of him. Was I in a bikie gang? No idea what you mean. Was I still dealing? I'm not dealing with this. Did I have guns? I flexed my biceps. Their good cop–bad cop routine was laughable.

A bloke in full uniform strode in. He looked high-ranking. 'I'm not sure you realise the trouble you're in, Simon. Your existing charge sheet is bad enough. And I see you breached your bail conditions again last week while we were looking for you. But all that's child's play compared to having an internal police document in your possession. There's nothing worse than an officer who abuses his position of trust. If the officer under investigation is associating with bikie gangs then a lot of people could be in serious danger. Forget your priors – for possessing that case file alone you're looking at five years. But if you cooperate with us then I promise we will provide the court with a letter of comfort, which will help enormously with the judge. So, let's start again. Who gave you the document?'

'What document?'

The DCC hammered his fist on the table. 'Simon, your fingerprints are all over these papers! What do you know about this man, Jack Bennett?' He pointed to a photo.

'Never seen him before.'

'Really? Well, is this you?' He pulled out a photo of me standing outside Bluey's house.

'Maybe.'

'And is this also you?' The next photo clearly showed me talking to Bennett.

'No comment.'

'And does this photo show Bennett handing these documents to you?'

'Can I see my solicitor, please?'

'Forget your solicitor. And forget ever seeing your dog again unless you cooperate. I'll be back in thirty minutes. Use them wisely.' He then told a uniformed officer to take me outside for a ciggie.

There was nowhere to turn. The evidence was undeniable. Investigators from Professional Standards had been tailing me ever since I started visiting Bluey, a known associate of Bennett's, who was already under investigation. The cops had assumed that I was a go-between for Bennett's bikie gang contacts because I rode a Harley. My only option was to agree to testify against him and take my chances in court. That made me a dog, on the wrong side of the gangland bosses and all the cops outside Professional Standards, who would no doubt close ranks to protect one of their own. I was neck deep in shit, way deeper than I'd ever imagined possible through dealing a few drugs. This was terrifying.

CHAPTER **TWELVE**

THE YELLOW Submarine, or 'The Sub' as the Melbourne Custody Centre on Lonsdale Street is widely known, is one of the most putrid jails on the planet. The notorious prisons of Turkey or Thailand could not be any more dehumanising. It's shameful that a developed country like Australia treats innocent people awaiting a bail decision like animals. But that's what happens when this type of service is contracted out to private companies that put profit before human rights.

Deep in the bowels of the Magistrates' Court, prisoners at The Sub are deprived of daylight and allowed only thirty minutes a day in the exercise area to stretch their legs. The centre is painted a sickly yellow – hence the name – and the bright fluorescent lighting enhances the nauseating effect. It's no wonder that everyone leaves looking jaundiced.

I was locked up there for four nights in a cell that measured about ten metres by six metres and slept six people. We had to shit in front of each other on a toilet with no seat. The stench was relentless. Every eight hours half a plastic container of dry fried rice or hard potatoes was poked through the slot in the metal door. Bed was a concrete slab with some crusty cushions and a blanket held together with the stains of a thousand previous inmates. There was just one pillow to go around which meant most of us just used our wet towels. My cellmates reeked of alcohol or were high on drugs. Many displayed fresh wounds from recent brawls. Nobody spoke a word, or even looked each other in the eye. I was still concussed and, without ice to release me from this new nightmare, I spent all my waking hours plunging deeper into despair.

Professional Standards didn't know what to do with me. They probably realised it wasn't safe for someone who was testifying against a bent cop to be locked up in the Melbourne Assessment Prison, another halfway house for anyone in the process of applying for bail. I might have been left to rot in The Sub if Vic hadn't answered Michelle's pleas for help and paid my barrister, Patrick Casey, to help me get bail. My brother, a Justice of the Peace and a pillar of the community, risked his own good name to help me out. That meant the world to me.

'Simon, when you are ready, please help me to help you,' he said to me when I got out. I would have burst into tears if I'd tried to respond, and a big bear hug spoke more than any words of thanks.

The strict bail conditions included participation in a Court Integrated Services Program, or CISP. This program provides specialised services like drug and alcohol counselling and mental health support in the hope that people won't reoffend. Fat chance of that. My other bail conditions included keeping away from Werribee and Hoppers Crossing. Vic said I could stay at his holiday home in Point Lonsdale, a small town west of Geelong on the Bellarine Peninsula. I had to sign in at the Geelong cop shop every day, observe a nightly curfew of 10 p.m. and attend a weekly session with my Corrections Victoria case worker.

I was glad to be out on bail, but the courts should have forced me into rehab. This was the perfect opportunity for intervention. My life was clearly fucked up. I was crying out for professional help and had no money for private treatment. It should've been obvious to everyone that I'd go straight back on the ice unless drastic measures were taken. The Sub made me feel sub-human and there was only one way to feel superhuman again. Within two hours of being released I'd smoked a gram.

The former addict who carried out my initial drug rehabilitation assessment took one look at the open sores on my face, which I constantly picked at when high, and said with a hint of admiration, 'Man, you've got it bad.' It soon became clear that their counsellors, experts in heroin, cocaine or alcohol addiction, knew next to nothing about ice. The drug was still too new at that time. I told them anything they wanted to hear so that I could finish up and go for a puff.

The mental health support was an even bigger joke. I was referred to the team covering the western suburbs, an area with a high immigrant population. The psychologists were often new to Australia themselves and spoke broken English. When my sixty minutes were up, even if I was pouring my heart out, I was abruptly shown the door. CISP could kiss my arse.

***

'LET ME see now,' said the duty sergeant as I waited at the front desk of the Geelong police station, ready to sign in for the day. 'Fenech. Yeah, thought I recognised that name. You're the cop dog, right? Taking one of our own down.'

'One of your own? So you're bent as well? Just give me the fucking sheet. I don't need this shit.'

'Think I haven't noticed the size of your pupils? Bigger than fucking Frisbees. I know your face now, snitch. You'd better watch your step out there.'

There was no point rising to the bait, although I thought it strange he didn't search me if he was so sure I'd been using. The encounter was a chilling reminder that I was stuck in a perilous no man's land until the Bennett case was sorted. I was on the wrong side of both the law and the local drug lords, although I was genuinely trying to keep my nose clean by concentrating on rebuilding my business. Bluey had found me a place where I could set up a makeshift factory and store my car parts – basically just a shed at the RAAF base at Laverton, a suburb east of Hoppers Crossing. He busted a gut helping me transport them from Dromana on his truck. I think it was a way of apologising for landing me in the shit by introducing me to Bennett. Nobody was buying my parts, though, and I had to resort to selling aluminium rims for scrap at $20 each to keep me in ice.

One night, about a month after my release from The Sub, I was driving through Norlane, near Geelong, on my way back to Point Lonsdale. I was breaking my curfew, driving unlicensed, and had half an eight ball in my glovebox. When I ran an amber light I heard a patrol car siren and saw the familiar blue and red flashing lights in my mirror. For a split second I thought about putting my foot down. But the last time hadn't worked out too well, so I pulled over and resigned myself to my fate.

'Can I see your licence please,' asked the officer.

'Don't have one.'

'What's your name and address?'

I told him and after he radioed in the information, he took my keys, told me to stay put and returned to his vehicle. About half an hour later two unmarked cars rolled up. I was shitting myself because I had no idea whose side they were on. I was cuffed and told to sit on the kerb while two detectives and one uniformed cop pulled the car to pieces. After about an hour one of the detectives took me aside.

'Driving unlicensed, breach of bail conditions, probably DUI. You know we should be locking you up, right?' My heart dropped into my sneakers. *Anything but The Sub again*, I thought. 'But I see you're due in court as a witness in a few weeks. Do me a favour, keep your head down until then, all right? And stay safe.'

That's it? No mention of the ice? There's no way they could have missed it. And then it all clicked into place. The real reason I'd been granted bail was because Professional Standards wanted me back on the streets in the hope that I'd lead them to Bennett's bosses. I'd probably been followed for the last month. And they wanted to follow me for another month, so they turned a blind eye to the ice and all the other offences. Knowing that I was being watched over, albeit for all the wrong reasons, was strangely reassuring.

***

ONE NIGHT, while Michelle's flatmate Tracie was out, we were spooning on the couch watching an episode of *CSI*. I wanted a puff, but Michelle had a rule about me not smoking in the flat.

'Aw, come on, I'll open the window,' I said.

'No, Simon. Go back to Point Lonsdale if you want one that badly. I wanted you to myself tonight, not share you with that stuff.'

'Okay, chill. You never minded me smoking my tits off when you were staying over at the factory. So don't get all high and mighty now. You know I'm not smoking anywhere near as much as I used to.'

'That's only because you're broke. Think of all the money that's literally gone up in smoke.'

'For fuck's sake, give me a break, eh? If you hadn't noticed, I've been having a pretty shit time of it lately. Is it too much to ask for you to work with me, not against me?'

'And is it too much to ask that our child doesn't have a junkie for a dad?'

Those words didn't make sense. She said 'our child'. No. Fucking. Way.

'What?' I said, unable to contain a smile. Somewhere, deep down, something inside me thought this was a good idea. 'Are you serious? You're pregnant?'

'Yep. Three months. Fancy sticking around and staying clean?'

At that moment all the decay that had been piling up around me just disintegrated. Hope, a feeling that had been long since buried, dared to resurface. If ever I needed an incentive to turn my life around, this was it. After my charges had been dealt with we could move away. Tasmania, perhaps. I could ship the spare parts down there and start afresh. Jake and Mackenzie could come visit. Michelle and I would work things out. She'd had my back while I was in The Sub and I'd really missed her when I took off to Mildura. Parenthood might smooth out our bumps. My mind often raced, but this time it was racing with clarity and purpose.

'Yeah, I really do fancy sticking around,' I told her.

Of course, within weeks things deteriorated. Michelle decided that I was going to play no part in the baby's life. She moved back to her sister's, changed her phone number and any hope of a new beginning was snuffed out, just as quickly as it had been ignited. That would be hard for anyone to cope with. For an addict it was catastrophic. I felt that I had no purpose in life. And nobody to turn to. I couldn't ask Vic to keep pulling me back from the brink. And my only mate, Axel, was caged in some council compound. I had reached my limit. The fighter was defeated.

***

WHEN THE sun's shining and the parks are full of picnicking families, Geelong's foreshore is as vibrant as anywhere in Australia. But when the wind rages in from Bass Strait and sheets of rain whip the pier, it's miserable. There, sitting in my parked car, I composed my final thoughts. I'd tried to contact Michelle earlier that afternoon but my call went to voicemail. That was the last straw. Now for the practicalities. First, I had to be off my face, otherwise I wouldn't have the guts to go through with it. The windows of the car fogged up as I smoked the last shards of half an eight ball. Next, I had to say goodbye to my brother.

Vic. No easy way 2 say this. Ive had enough, brother. This is no life 4 me. Dont think bad of me. You did all u could but I want 2 be with Dad Mum and Dave now. Will always love you.
Simon

I left the message in Drafts on my phone. I'd send it when I got back to Port Lonsdale.

Finally, I had to explain it to the kids. When I scribbled the words down in pencil in an A4 spiral notebook, it made even more sense.

Jake and Mackenzie
Please, always know that your dad loves you. But I'm not the dad I want to be for you both. I have made some terrible mistakes and life has become too hard for me. Honestly, you are both better off without me around. Don't feel sad because I will be with Nannu, Nanna and Uncle Dave. Look after your mum and listen to everything she tells you. She is a good woman. Remember, I love you both more than you can imagine and I will always be looking down on you.
Dad xxx

The drive back to Point Lonsdale took about forty minutes on empty roads. I could barely see through the rain-lashed windscreen and my tears. I parked under the carport, pulled the shotgun out from the side of the driver's seat, and threw my road pipe and empty bags into the wheelie bin. Once inside the house I went straight to my bedroom and switched on the bedside lamp. I tore the sheet out of the notebook and placed it on the bedside table, underneath my favourite picture of Jake and Mackenzie, all gap-toothed smiles.

Next to the bed was an old military ammunition box containing around a hundred red shotgun cartridges. Sure of my path, I'd picked up the ammo the previous day. The brass head on one cartridge seemed newer and shinier than the rest. Fortunately, the gauge matched the bore of my double-trigger Winchester. I opened the barrel breach lever, bent the gun open, loaded the cartridge into the left barrel and snapped it shut. After leaning the gun against the wall I sent the text message to Vic.

I then sat on the edge of the bed and wedged the stock against my knee. Sobbing, I trialled the best position; under my chin, inside my mouth or to the side of my head. There seemed to be the least chance of something going wrong with the gun inside my mouth, so I released the safety catch. The rough, sawn-off ends scraped against the roof of my mouth.

Then I squeezed the trigger.

CHAPTER **THIRTEEN**

STRONG HANDS under armpits and around ankles. Spitting blood. Horrible taste. Ears ringing. Nosebleed. Roof of mouth shredded. What the fuck's going on?

'How ya doing, soldier?' asked a uniformed cop. He and his partner were dragging me backwards out of Vic's house through the front door, which had been kicked off its hinges. 'Don't be doing this again in a hurry, eh? Somebody would've had to clean up a lot of brain if you'd actually put ammo in the gun.' They manoeuvred me onto the edge of the back seat of their patrol car and told me to lie down. I was disorientated, but the shock of being alive was swamped by the realisation that I hadn't thought about the poor bastard who might have found me with my head blown to pieces.

'What do you mean about the ammo?' I moaned.

'That cartridge might have scared a few cockies from the paddock, but it wasn't ideal for what you had in mind. You're still fucking lucky, though. Trust me, I do a fair bit of shooting. Your gun was too powerful and the over powder wad got stuck in the barrel. The blast knocked you out, but it would have been a lot messier if the projectile had actually fired.'

'What the hell you were doing with a sawn-off is a different matter altogether,' said his partner. 'We're going to have to report that, obviously. But you need help, mate. Do us all a favour and talk to your brother, eh? Victor rang us as soon as he got your text. He's going to meet us at the hospital. He's really worried about you.'

Talking to Vic would not be easy. I now had the added shame of having tried to take the coward's way out. How could I look him in the face? He might well have found my body. How could he have ever set foot in that house again? *You selfish cunt,* I told myself and was relieved when the cop car pulled in at the reception of the Swanston Centre psychiatric unit of Geelong's hospital instead of the Emergency Department. *Finally, a chance of proper treatment. These guys will know what to do with me.* I expected to be admitted for a full psychiatric evaluation. Instead, I had a fifteen-minute chat with a junior doctor. I felt like I'd been chewing razor blades and there was congealed blood in my ears. I could barely hear the guy let alone answer his questions. I was eventually told that there was nothing they could do because I was already on a mental health plan. After reassuring them that I wouldn't try to harm myself again they let me go with a couple of Valium and a bottle of mouthwash.

***

'WHAT THE hell were you thinking, Simon?' Vic barked as he drove me from the hospital. He'd offered to put me up for a few nights on the condition that I stayed away from ice. I couldn't blame him for being wary of me. He'd only recently learnt of the full list of charges that I was facing and it probably freaked him out. I wasn't good for his reputation. And his priority was the wellbeing of his family; his wife and daughters and his brother-in-law, who was suffering with cancer and had recently moved in. That was a measure of the man, he'd do anything for anybody. It was up to me to earn his trust all over again. 'I know you're suffering, brother, but think of Jake and Mackenzie. You may not realise it, but they still worship you. No child can deal with their dad taking his own life, and in such a brutal way. It can really damage a child.'

'It's not just Jake and Mackenzie now; Michelle's carrying my baby,' I mumbled.

'Wow! So there you go. This is the crossroads for you. You can't turn back and you can't keep making wrong turns. The only way is forward and that means leaving all this drug shit behind. New baby, new start. What you tried to do tonight stays between you and me, okay? But you have to promise me you'll never try anything like that again.'

I gave Vic my word, for what it was worth.

***

AFTER A couple of days at Vic's I needed my own space again, and I needed some gear. So I threw a mattress down in my shed at Laverton, chained Betty up outside on a rope that gave her the run of the yard, and welcomed back a few old customers who came both for car parts and for drugs. One young bloke turned up with a slim blonde girl called Becca who had a calm, reassuring nature. She opened me up like a surgeon, massaged my fragile heart, and then pieced me back together. Becca was better than any counsellor. She was the shoulder to cry on that I sorely needed, even though we were incompatible as a couple. Within a month she was also pregnant.

Drugs like ice leave a trail of hopeless, loveless unions. I fell all too easily into the arms of anyone who paid me a bit of attention or showed me the slightest bit of affection. I suppose the loss of my parents, as well as the brother who best understood my troubles, had destroyed the very foundations of my existence. I was emotionally marooned and didn't feel able to turn to family for comfort or guidance. I convinced myself I wouldn't have been in this mess if Dad had been alive. And Mum was no longer there to soak up my hurt with a warm hug. I'd forgotten how to form meaningful attachments, and ice-fuelled sex is the poorest of substitutes for love.

Three years earlier, Becca had gone full-term before her baby was stillborn. The doctors told her that she'd never fall pregnant again. She was devastated, so this pregnancy felt like a miracle. Deep down, I knew that I was in no condition to be a father to two new babies, but I'd been man enough to make the babies and so I was determined to do whatever I could. Michelle was due in three months but we hadn't been in contact and I wasn't sure what role I'd be allowed to play. Becca's pregnancy seemed to be another lifeline, a fresh incentive to turn things around, and I made a real effort to cut down on the ice and focus on my bail programs. I was also determined that both Michelle and Becca should know about my life before I was messed up. I wasn't convinced that I'd be around for long enough to tell my kids that I'd once been a decent man.

Becca was pretty chilled, but sometimes I found this infuriating. One day I asked her to help me move a car from Laverton over to a customer. It was unregistered, so I had to take it on the back of the truck, which was also unregistered. Not only that, the brake lights didn't work. Rain was coming down and darkness was closing in. Becca's job was to drive behind me so that any cops couldn't spot the dodgy rego plate and the faulty brake lights. At some point on the journey she decided to clear off and do her own thing. When my truck broke down at the side of the road, she was nowhere to be found. I was stranded until she finally answered her phone and came to pick me up, two hours later.

'Where the fuck have you been?' I snarled, climbing into the passenger seat.

'Oh, just thought I'd stop and have a quick manicure,' she said, proudly showing off her bright red, lacquered nails.

'I do not fucking believe I'm hearing this,' I said, scrunching myself down into the seat and screwing myself into a tight ball. 'I've been waiting here like a dick for hours, shitting myself that the cops could pull up at any time. You know how edgy I am at the moment. And you're getting your fucking nails done? What were you thinking? Are you trying to get me locked up?'

'Take it easy, man. You sound fucked in the head.'

'You think I'm fucked in the head? You think I'm fucking fucked in the head? I'll show you fucked in the head.' With that, I thrust my right foot up into the windscreen. It shuddered but held firm. Humiliated, I kicked out again, harder. This time cracks appeared. One more, and my foot went clean through. If it had been the back windscreen the whole thing would have shattered and caved in. But the laminated screen held firm around the hole and, when I pulled my foot out, the glass sliced straight through my Achilles tendon with an audible ping. I lifted my leg off the glass and blood gushed out. The untethered calf muscle had contracted up towards my knee joint and the pain was ten times worse than cramp.

'See what I mean, you're fucked in the head,' Becca said, as calm as you like.

'Just get a rag from the truck and there's some electrical tape in the back,' I said. 'And be quick.' I managed to wrap the rag tightly above the wound, staunching the blood flow, and secured it with the tape. Then I hopped round to the driver's side and told Becca to make her own way home. Even with one leg, I'd be able to drive quicker than her. Using my left leg to operate both the accelerator and brake pedals, I managed to negotiate the four or five kilometres to Werribee Hospital in just a few minutes. I swear that some of the staff rolled their eyes when I stumbled through the doors, bloodied and desperate for help yet again. On this occasion I was transferred to Footscray Hospital where the two ends of the tendon were stitched together under general anaesthetic. Becca visited during my four-day recovery, but was understandably distant. Would having me in her baby's life be worth this kind of hassle? Of course not. The chance of this child being part of my salvation was already looking like a twisted fantasy.

***

THE TIMING of this latest injury wasn't ideal. After two weeks on crutches I was able to hobble around with the help of a moon boot, but I could only wear gym shorts – not a good look for my big day in court. Becca wasn't the type to sit patiently through a long and boring hearing, so I took the bus into the city and limped over to a bench in the corridor outside the designated court, where I'd agreed to meet my barrister, Patrick.

I was shitting myself that I was heading back behind bars. The long list of charges – possession of illegal firearms, dealing ice, possession of stolen goods, and traffic offences which carried fines totalling tens of thousands of dollars – portrayed me as someone the cops would definitely want off the streets. Fortunately, although the dirty cop Jack Bennett had recently pleaded guilty to charges including misconduct in public office, theft of ice from Fitzroy police station and attempting to pervert the course of justice, my letter of comfort from the cops was still valid even though I hadn't been called on to give evidence. Would it be enough to keep me out of jail, though? If it didn't, would Bennett's connections inside prison make an example of me for agreeing to testify?

Patrick pulled out all the stops arguing my case. He stressed that I'd suffered family tragedies, that I'd never touched ice until my work accident, that I used to be a hardworking family man, and that I had a kid on the way. (Nobody else knew about Becca's baby at that point.) Then the court was cleared so that the letter from Professional Standards could be read to the judge, confirming that I'd been willing to cooperate. It was all very cloak and dagger. Patrick believed this was the ace up my sleeve.

The judge, who spoke like his mouth was full of marbles, thought otherwise.

'Stand up, Fenech,' he said. 'Your catalogue of charges is an absolute disgrace and you have shown no remorse for your constant offending. As such, in my mind, you are a danger to yourself and a menace to society. What I have heard today convinces me that you have no regard for the efforts of the police to uphold the laws of this land. You were adamant that you would not help police investigate the men who attacked you at your factory. So the fact that you were willing to testify against a serving police officer does not impress me in the slightest. In fact, I see this as an act of opportunism, calculated to serve your own ends and to exact some sort of perverse revenge against an officer of the law. To use your own colourful language, this is the act of a dog. However, to some extent my hands are tied by the law and I am forced to consider non-custodial options, although I am far from convinced that this is the best option. I therefore sentence you to two corrections orders of eighteen months each, starting one week apart. Think yourself lucky, Fenech, and mark my words, this is your very last chance.'

I didn't know whether to laugh or cry. The good news was that I wasn't going to prison. But had a judge just called me a dog for cooperating with the police? And a menace to society? I left the courtroom more broken than if I'd been sentenced to fifty lashes.

'That fucker's set me up to fail,' I told Vic outside the court. 'Two corrections orders running at the same time? That means two lots of community service, two lots of drug counselling, two mental health programs. Nobody can stick to that, especially without a driver's licence. He wants me to screw up so that he can lock me up next time.'

'Next time?' Vic asked, with a resigned sigh. 'The whole point is that there won't be a next time.'

***

MICHELLE'S DUE date came and went. Knowing that I had another kid out there, but not knowing anything about it, was crucifying me. Somehow Michelle controlled the silence of her friends and family with military precision. Nothing was posted on social media and nobody would answer my calls. Part of me respected her decision. Perhaps this child, like Jake and Mackenzie, was better off without me. Meanwhile, Becca's pregnancy was progressing well and I tried to do my bit by decorating a nursery at her house, and shopping for groceries and baby clothes. Our relationship was never hot and cold like with Michelle, more like a friendship based on shared responsibility. I could imagine a long-term role in this baby's life.

For that reason, I'd been trying to sort myself out and my ice use was down to a new low. The corrections orders and community service took up most of my time. I had to remove graffiti from fences and walls with a high-pressure cleaning system; walk up to twelve kilometres a day picking up rubbish; and paint park benches or outdoor equipment. On rainy days we unpicked the stitches of embroidered patches on workmen's clothing so that the tops could be resold in op shops. My fingers were too fat to even grip the pickers, testing my fragile patience. I craved a puff to relax me and to relieve the tedium.

Running the spare parts business was no longer possible and, in any case, I had to get away from that world. Money was tight, and when I was kicked out of the makeshift factory in Laverton for not paying rent I had to move all my remaining cars and parts to a farm in Melton owned by a friend of my brother, Dave. I also needed a place to stay and so I rented a room in a large shared house in Hoppers Crossing.

Out of the blue, Michelle called. 'Do you want to see your son?'

'Wait, what? You had a little boy? I have a son? Of course I want to see him! When? Today's good. Where?'

'Easy, easy. This doesn't change anything. I just think it's only right that you meet him. His name's Brodie, by the way.'

We met in a park the following day and my heart melted when I set eyes on the little fella, all cocooned in his baby capsule. He had the squidgy Fenech nose. Finally, there was new life to celebrate amid all the death and misery. While he cooed and gurgled, I bawled like a baby. I half-hoped that Michelle would allow me into Brodie's life on a regular basis. She did agree to the occasional visit but the volatility between us soon resurfaced when she found out about Becca. Michelle had wrongly suspected something had been going on before we split up. Any meaningful truce would be tough to maintain.

Moving into that house in Hoppers Crossing, owned by a skinny and likeable bloke called Zippo, was a big mistake. His story mirrored mine in many ways. He first tried ice after injuring his back while working as a butcher and our shared history was the subject of many a heart-to-heart over a puff. All the other guys who rented rooms were on ice as well and the temptation to join them was too great. The self-control I'd exercised while performing my corrections orders went out the window.

Within a few weeks of my court case, and possibly because the cops were still keeping a careful eye on me, I was pulled over. I'd already been warned that I was in the last chance saloon, so this new charge of driving while disqualified – an instant breach of both corrections orders – would be frowned upon by the courts. What was the point in continuing to make an effort to turn things around if jail was inevitable? My life was starting to unravel again. Michelle was disillusioned with me and Becca kept me at arms' length after she started receiving anonymous phone calls warning her not to associate with the 'cop dog'. Old sores festered in that diseased environment.

A return to dealing was the easy fall-back option. But the ice we were smoking at Zippo's was shit. Nobody bought it on a regular basis. One of Zippo's hangers-on, Blacky, who had flesh tunnels in his earlobes bigger than hula hoops, suggested that I visit a cook house in Bacchus Marsh. I agreed.

The place looked like every other ice den, which was worrying in itself. I expected more secrecy. The cook, a Russian bloke with an ugly red knot of scar tissue where his right eye should have been, met us at the door and led us to a locked garage at the rear of the property. Even outside, the air stank of ammonia. Inside was a grungy assortment of beakers, Bunsen burners, flasks, condensers, funnels, pipettes and test tubes. Containers of chemicals were stored at the back of the garage in a pool of their contents. Unused cordless drills were piled in one corner, the lithium extracted from their batteries. Countless empty plastic bottles of drain cleaner and paint thinner littered the floor. Hundreds of matchbooks were carelessly discarded, with the striker strips scratched off with razor blades to collect red phosphorous. This guy had clearly tried every method for cooking meth.

Whoa! This is scary shit and way out of my league, I told myself. *There's some serious jail time in this garage. I don't want a bar of this.*

'You know hypo?' the Russian asked.

'Yeah, I know of it,' I replied cautiously. He meant hypo-phosphorous acid, which I knew was in short supply and fetched around $3 a millilitre. It was one of the chemicals that could be used to extract meth from common over-the-counter products containing pseudoephedrine.

'You get me some? Get me hypo, and I give you best gear.'

'Let me make some enquiries,' I said, lying through my teeth. 'Can I ask you one question?'

'Sure, fire away. No secrets here.'

'Why is there a condom on top of that tube?'

'This is for safety. When condom inflate, too much phosphine gas. When too much phosphine gas, tube explode. When tube explode, you lose eye.' He burst into a fit of evil-genius cackling.

'Get me the fuck out of here, fast,' I whispered to Blacky, who looked shocked and offended that his entrepreneurial efforts had been thwarted.

Soon after, Blacky told me that he'd found a dealer with amazing gear. I cautiously agreed to check it out but I was down to my last grand and didn't trust Blacky as far as I could throw him. To reassure me, he said he'd meet me in a side street in St Albans, a suburb north-west of Sunshine, and buy the gear while I watched.

As soon as I arrived he changed his story. 'The dealer's spooked,' he said. 'He wants me to go alone. It's only round the corner. I'll literally be gone for two minutes. Trust me, his gear's worth it.'

Half an hour later I was still waiting and was convinced that the fucker had run off with my money. Then he reappeared with my eight ball. He didn't want to stick around for a puff, so it wasn't a surprise when the gear turned out to be dog shit. As I tried it out, fuming about the quality, a car with two Asians inside pulled up alongside mine and the passenger wound his window down.

'You want gear?' he said.

'Nah, just bought some.'

'From Blacky?'

'Yeah, it's fucking shit.'

'Not fucking shit. That my gear.'

'Then you've ripped me off, because it's shit.'

'Blacky rip you off, not me. He cut. My gear best in town.' That's why the bastard had taken half an hour, I realised. 'You ring me next time. Put on speed dial. I come here quick.'

Back at Zippo's the others were stoked to hear that I had access to a main man. I easily managed to scrape together another grand for an eight ball. I rang the bloke's number but was told that a quarter was the minimum order. We needed another grand, but word was spreading fast, and the extra money was quickly found. I arranged to meet the Asian dealer in the same spot two days later and, for the first time ever in the history of dealing ice, he turned up on time.

'Throw money,' he said. I lobbed the roll of notes into his car and fully expected to smell burning rubber as he screeched off down the street. But no. He removed the elastic band, quickly counted the cash and then threw a bag of ice through my window. 'See you next time my friend. Remember, speed dial,' he added and laughed as they pulled away.

This shard was a vision of purity – almost glacier-blue in its transparency, with ruler-straight edges. And it was dynamite to smoke. Clean-tasting, long-lasting, pure-puffing, mind-blowing dynamite. When word got out, users flocked from miles around, drooling in anticipation. The vampires even came out in the daylight. Demand went through the roof. I had to call Speed Dial that very night to pick up another quarter. Next time, I bought half an ounce for $4000. Even though the price of a point was down to around $50 by then, fourteen grams had a street value of $7000. But selling the odd point here and there wasn't worth the effort. People were willing to pay $4000 up front for half a bag (half an ounce or fourteen grams).

This was a different clientele compared to the users who had to rob and steal for their next hit. These people were white-collar workers with responsible jobs who bought their ice on Thursday or Friday in preparation for the weekend. Saturday, when they smoked it, was often a quiet day and then they'd come shuffling back on Sunday for enough to see them through the start of another working week. I managed to run a business in the early stages of my addiction but these people took high-functioning addiction to a whole new level. My customers included a police officer, drug counsellors, staff at the Department of Human Services, a vet and two teachers. It was hard to imagine how someone could operate on a pet budgie or teach a chemistry lesson on this gear. And, of course, my customers were only a tiny scratch on the surface of the ice epidemic. Half of Australia was hooked.

Before long I was buying one-ounce bags for $7000 and making a decent clip as the middleman. There was just one – major – problem. I was spending all my money on an addiction that'd escalated to a frightening new level in a very short time. Previously, five or six points a day was enough. Now I was smoking four or five *grams* a day – ten times as much. And I felt ten times as desperate.

CHAPTER **FOURTEEN**

'SIMON, THIS is Becca's mum. She's gone into labour. We're at Werribee Hospital. She's quite well dilated, so you should hurry. Let me know when you get this message, please, because she's asking for you.'

There was no point in replying, I'd be there in a quarter of an hour, even with a quick stop at a servo for some flowers. I was jittery with anticipation. It'd been almost ten years since I'd witnessed Mackenzie being born. This time I'd barely known the mother for ten months. *How affectionate should I be? Should I be at the business end? Would I cry, as I'd done when both Jake and Mackenzie were born?*

The moaning and wailing from the depths of the labour ward reminded me of my previous visits. The noise sends shivers down the spines of all prospective parents. The receptionist directed me to Becca's room, which seemed almost tranquil in comparison. She was in discomfort, but not agony.

'I came as soon as I got your mum's message,' I said. 'How's it going, girl? Got you these.' I handed her the bunch of wilting yellow flowers, which were batted to the floor as another contraction gripped.

'You must be the father,' said the midwife. 'Everything seems to be going smoothly. Eight centimetres dilated. Shouldn't be long now.'

I pulled up a seat and offered my hand as a sacrifice.

Within half an hour, Becca, normally so relaxed, was out-screaming the whole ward. Somehow she found the strength to fling me down to the bottom of the bed to watch our baby being delivered.

It was obvious straight away something was wrong. With Jake and Mackenzie there had been an explosion of vibrant colour – reds, pinks and the deep blue of the umbilical cord. This time the colours were pastel, almost grey. *Why's the baby not crying? Or moving?* The midwife and nurses couldn't hide their concern, and one called for a specialist while the cord was cut and unwrapped from around the baby girl's neck. Becca didn't even have a chance to hold her daughter before the baby was taken to the neonatal unit.

'Somebody tell me what's happening,' she cried. 'Where's Charlie being taken?'

The nurses tried to reassure her but it's almost impossible to calm a mother who has already suffered one stillbirth. Too exhausted to maintain the intensity of her own distress, she collapsed into her mother's embrace.

I just froze. I may have hugged Becca. I may have wiped her brow. I may have held her hand. I have no memory of those moments. But I was no support, I know that much.

After an agonising hour or so, a specialist arrived to deliver the news. 'I'm afraid it doesn't look good. Charlie's brain was starved of oxygen for quite some time while the cord was around her neck. Her brain has been badly damaged and she can't breathe without assistance. Her heartbeat is also very weak. She's going to be transferred to the Monash Children's Hospital, where she will be in the best hands. But she is extremely poorly and you should prepare yourselves for the worst. Mum, I expect you'll want to be travelling in the ambulance with Charlie. Dad and Grandma might want to have a quick look at her beforehand.'

The doctors and nurses were frantically fussing around the incubator and it was difficult to see her through all the wires and tubes. That was my last glimpse of Charlie.

***

I COULDN'T bring myself to go back to the hospital and witness her struggle. Instead, I shut down. I withdrew into the room I was renting, closed the curtains and locked the door. For five days I fried my brain with ice. The same questions repeatedly hammered me. *Was this my fault? Was it God's punishment for all my mistakes? Were the deaths of my family not enough? Why take an innocent baby girl, too? Where's the wisdom? Where's the mercy? What kind of god would do that?* And the answer to that question was unavoidable. *No god would do that.* I lost all faith, and faith had been one of my few brittle crutches.

The only messages I responded to were from Becca. The outcome was inevitable. Charlie would never be able to breathe on her own and her brain was severely damaged. After six days came the message that no parent should ever receive. The doctors had requested permission to turn off Charlie's life support. Becca pleaded with me to go to the hospital to say my goodbyes, to hug and hold Charlie for the first and last time. Her mother explained to her that I was 'saturated with death'. This was true. But what kind of man cowers when the life that he has created is about to be extinguished? Only a hopeless addict, totally detached from all moral obligation.

***

THE DAYS leading up to the funeral passed in a fog of self-pity. I fixated on how I was going to end it all after Charlie was buried. These thoughts were my only solace. By cutting myself off from the outside world I could limit the damage that I caused to others. Vic didn't even know Charlie existed. Becca's dad bought a coffin and a hospital charity paid for the other expenses. All I had to do was turn up.

Wearing my black suit and a black tie, I parked at the Altona Memorial Park cemetery. The other mourners were mainly from Becca's family, although a few of my associates from the ice community showed, which was unusual. As sceptical as ever, I suspected it was to see if I had any of the new gear on me. Becca spotted me arrive, walked over and linked her arm in mine. I was already a mess of tears, as was she.

Then I saw Charlie's burial place, flanked by sheets of synthetic grass draped over wooden boards surrounding the grave. It was so small, but so deep. The priest came over to shake my hand and asked if I wanted to carry the coffin to the grave. I nodded, but couldn't see a hearse. He pointed to a silver Rolls-Royce, parked about thirty metres away. Still linked to Becca, I trudged over and saw the tiny pink coffin on the back seat. This was too much to bear and we both broke down again.

'Come on, we have to do this,' wept Becca, placing her arm around my shoulder.

The coffin felt so tiny and weightless, yet every step of that walk to the graveside was agonising. Two funeral directors, one on each side, stood by the straps that would be used to lower the coffin. I crouched down on my haunches with one hand on the coffin, unable to pull away. Becca placed a hand on my shoulder, the signal to let our daughter go. As I stood up, I reached into my pants pocket for a tissue and, when I pulled it out, a big bag of ice fell onto the fake grass. I picked it up and stuffed it in my jacket pocket as the other mourners looked on, incredulous. My mortification was complete.

CHAPTER **FIFTEEN**

I VISITED Charlie's grave every other day for the next two weeks. I felt drawn to her and there was a strange peace to be found in the children's section of the cemetery. Among the whirling, plastic windmills and the cuddly toys adorning the other graves, I believed that Charlie was not alone. My broken mind played tricks on me. If I listened carefully I could hear the squeals and chatter of children at play. Talking to her seemed natural. I asked if her sister, the baby from Becca's previous pregnancy, was looking after her. I asked if her Nannu, Nanna and Uncle Dave had found her. And I asked if she'd like me to join her.

***

THE TRIPS to the cemetery should have been a tonic, but instead they were a painful reminder of what I was missing out on. I obediently stuck to my corrections orders appointments, while casually breaching them whenever I drove to meet Speed Dial. I dealt only enough to make sure that I was never short. Sometimes I just needed a change of scenery and drove around without apparent purpose or a known destination. My subconscious had been poisoned and I could no longer analyse my own intentions. I didn't realise that I was tempting something, anything, to bring a stop to this endless cycle of despair. Then, about three weeks after Charlie's death, an opportunity to do just that presented itself.

I'd been scheduled for a late-afternoon session with a psychologist whom my counsellor had described as the best in Melbourne when it came to addiction. But for three-quarters of the appointment the doctor fretted that she hadn't received the court paperwork necessary to trigger her payment. The prospect of progress was wasted, another glimmer of hope snuffed out. This fresh despair prompted me to drive around for hours in one of the unregistered cars that were always on hand at Zippo's. Eventually I found myself on the West Gate Freeway where I ran out of petrol. I managed to crawl onto the hard shoulder just before the Kororoit Creek turn-off near Laverton. I had no money and my phone was dead. In any case, who could I have called? Nobody stopped to help.

I slumped over the steering wheel and convinced myself that this was it. Nothing had changed since my last attempt to kill myself. Things were actually worse. *Do you have the guts to try again?* The answer must have been 'yes', although I didn't feel in control. In my rear-view mirror I spotted the powerful headlights of a flat-nose truck approaching and got out of the car. When the truck was around thirty metres away, maybe more, I took two deliberate steps onto the road. I heard the screech of locked brakes. Then the horn. I smelt smoking tyres. *This is the end.* I closed my eyes and tensed. The impact was thunderous. I felt air whistle past my ears and landed on my back, smacking my head hard against the asphalt. *Silence.* Opening my eyes, the Mercedes badge on the grill behind the shiny bull bars was a metre away. The tail section had jack-knifed around towards me and the rear brake lights pierced the smoke from the burnt rubber.

I'm not dead? I'm actually not dead? So what now? You can't face the poor fucker whose life you've just ruined. I sat up and then cautiously stood. The back of my head was bleeding and my legs were like jelly, but all my bones seemed intact. I took a couple of tentative steps and then, hunched over like a monkey to protect my battered right side, stumbled towards the exit ramp and away from the shouts behind me. When I was far enough away, and confident that I wasn't being followed, I glanced back to see two or three people gathered around the driver, who was gesturing and pointing animatedly in my direction.

After the adrenaline burst, I felt weak and nauseous and wanted to take myself off the streets in case anyone came looking for me. I knew the labyrinth of roads around that junction and headed for an old haunt, The Tarmac Hotel, where there was a strong chance that somebody might owe me a favour. Sure enough, the guy on the first pokie machine inside the front door was a former customer.

'Fuck, Simon, you look shit, mate. What happened? You look like you've been hit by a truck. Let me take you home.'

***

KILLING MYSELF shouldn't have been so hard. The tough part was supposed to be the decision. A pattern was starting to develop, though. Both suicide attempts had resulted in me licking new wounds, not ending my torment. In my mind I was convinced that I'd had enough. But was my mind, taken hostage by ice, a reliable judge? Was I really seeking closure, or a gateway for help? I hadn't told anyone about the latest suicide attempt, so I certainly didn't seem to be looking for sympathy. *No mistakes next time.*

As soon as I was able to drag myself off the bed, I smoked the rest of my stash, at least a gram of the good stuff. Ashamed of the trauma I'd already caused innocent people such as Vic, the coppers and the truck driver, I waited until the house was empty in the early hours of the morning. The others were probably out chasing deals. I snuck into the garage which was packed to the rafters with stolen goods that I'd accepted in exchange for shard. Ironically, I'd only recently flogged the last of a batch of ten mahogany coffins. In my circles, coffins were an easy sell. Even the roll of blue nylon rope I held now, no thicker than my thumb, was knocked off.

Two sturdy wooden roof beams ran from one wall to the other and, after throwing the rope over one beam, I made a noose by following a video on my phone. I tied the other end to the bumper of my GT ute, the one vehicle the cops had returned because I'd proved that it wasn't the proceeds of crime with an eBay paper trail. Then I carried a sturdy coffee table from inside the house and turned it on its side. It would take my weight comfortably and I'd easily be able to topple it over at the final moment. There was no note, no text message. That way, I felt detached from the consequences. But I wanted one last ciggie. There was no more ice to smoke and, in any case, I couldn't have been any higher so there'd be minimal pain. A cigarette was more symbolic – the traditional last request of the condemned man.

I was weeping when I lit up, sobbing halfway through and, as I took another drag, climbing onto the table and sliding the noose over my neck, wailing from the very depths of my being. One more drag, followed by the slightest shift in balance, and it would all be over. Then a car pulled up in the drive. I froze, torn between what I was about to do and the thought of subjecting the driver, probably Zippo, to the horror of finding my body. I howled with an intensity I'd only once heard before, when the heroin addict mother discovered that she'd killed her baby.

***

ZIPPO UNTIED the rope from the bumper, helped me down from the table and unravelled the noose. We talked, I cried, we smoked. He was shocked and genuinely worried. The other people living at the house drifted back throughout the night. They showed fleeting concern, then asked when they could place their next orders. Zippo packed me off to bed as dawn broke, convinced that a new day would bring me a fresh outlook and renewed support.

When I woke in the afternoon, reclusive and embarrassed, my phone was filled with anxious messages. Vic offered to come and talk; Becca put aside her own grief; Michelle wanted me to spend quality time with Brodie that day.

For fuck's sake, snap out of it, I told myself. *Talk to these people. Do the corrections orders. Make some money from dealing. Keep your head down. Find a place to live, away from all this shit. Ditch the drugs. Learn to trust again, to love again. And time will heal.*

Such moments of self-awareness were rare. As more customers bought Speed Dial's product, the more I used myself, eager to share their experience. When high, I couldn't focus on the next few minutes let alone the next few years. But although I smoked all day every day, I still had to keep my wits about me. New customers had to be vouched for and vetted. When two Middle Eastern–looking guys that I hadn't seen before pulled into the driveway in a shiny BMW, car stereo pounding out beats, alarm bells rang. From the side door I gestured irritably for them to turn the volume down.

'Are you Simon?' A muscly bloke with a shaved head and a cross tattooed under his eye strode towards me with the swagger of someone who'd just had a fresh puff. 'We're here to buy some gear. Half a bag.'

'Sorry, don't know what you're talking about.'

'C'mon, man. Zack told us you'd be cool. Told us your gear was the duck's nuts.'

'Okay, but keep your fucking voice down and come inside.' I led them into the garage through the inside door. Why hadn't Zack said anything? 'Stay there while I go and get it. It'll be seven grand.' I kept my gear in my locked bedroom, changing the hiding place regularly. When I came back, I took one step into the garage and the two skunks, positioned either side of the door, both raised military-style 9-millimetre pistols with dual magazines to my head.

'Check if he's carrying,' the older one ordered. With his spare hand, and without taking his eyes off mine, the younger one frisked my legs and around my waist. It was obvious there was nothing concealed under my T-shirt. But he stopped at my front jeans pocket, which contained a $10,000 roll of notes.

'Pleased to see me?' he sniggered. 'Hand it over. Give me the ice, too.'

This was no time for heroics, even if nearly $20,000 was disappearing before my eyes. I handed him the bag.

'Show us where you keep the rest. And your cash,' barked the older one.

'One, that's all I have. Two, there are five other blokes in there. That's six of us to your two. Use your fucking brain. You got more than you expected, now fuck off.'

The older bloke mulled this over. 'Okay, here's how this'll work from here. Open the roller door, then stay still and we're out of here.' They backed out of the garage. The door switch was next to me and I did as he asked. Then they edged towards the car, guns still trained on me.

'Put the fucking guns down, you fuckwits. People can see you. You've got what you came for, now fuck off.'

With smug grins on their faces, they climbed into the BMW. The young one slammed it in reverse, screeched to a stop on the road and then roared off down the street.

***

THE PROSPECT of constantly looking over my shoulder was wearying. I'd just started to feel as though the heat was off me.

But I'd put this particular target on my back by keeping control of the distribution of the good gear. Every time I left Zippo's, I was worried that I'd be robbed. I considered buying another gun but then thought of something else. Ever since Axel was impounded, I'd been challenging the authorities to release him. The council wanted to put him down because he was an American pit bull, a restricted breed. But I tried to claim he was half Amstaff (American staffy) and half Hungarian Vizsla. More to the point, he'd never attacked anyone. It tortured me to think of my best mate caged and wondering why his dad had deserted him. I was desperate to give him a cuddle and reassure him that he'd be out soon. I was also in need of the kind of no-strings affection that only a dog could provide. But the bastards wouldn't even tell me where he was being kept.

'Look, mate, I'm trying to be reasonable here. I'm not going to try and bust my dog out, I just want to visit him,' I told the local dog ranger on the phone. 'You've no idea how much he means to me right now. I'm not in a good place. I really need to see my dog or I'm scared what I'll do.'

'Is that a threat, Mr Fenech? I'm telling you it's council policy not to reveal that information. My hands are tied.'

'Yeah, it was a threat. But not against you. It was against me.' I was hyperventilating and furious. 'Your hands are tied, right? So here's what will happen to my hands if you don't show some humanity. I'm going to come down to the council offices this afternoon, chop off one of my hands with an axe in front of everyone and spray the walls with my blood. What's your fucking council policy for that?'

The dog ranger hung up and I punched a hole through my

bedroom wall. *Fuck this. I can't take any more. Tonight's the night. No mistakes this time.*

Again I smoked myself numb. And in that state, when planning and strategy are impenetrable languages, I chose a method that would require minimal courage. Poor Zippo would probably be the person to find me. What did I care? More than likely he'd be off his head. Once again I waited until the house was empty, this time in the late evening. I went into the garage, grabbed two vacuum cleaner hoses and jammed them in the GT's twin exhausts. I wrapped two towels around the junctions of hose and exhaust to make a tight seal, then ran the hoses through the car windows. Next, I wound up the windows and stuffed more towels into the gaps to prevent the fumes from escaping. No cigarettes this time, the last drag had been too confronting before. And this time my emotions were totally different. I was defeated, resigned to my fate. I sat in the driver's seat, closed the door and turned on the ignition.

Fuck, it gets smoky fast . . .

There are two explanations for what happened next but to this day I don't know which is more credible. One hour later, maybe two, maybe three, I regained consciousness on the garage floor. The engine had stopped but the dash lights were still on. There was a new bump on the back of my head. My breath tasted disgusting. The air in the garage was misty.

At some point the car had run out of petrol. At some other point, whether before or after is not clear, I'd opened the car door and fallen out of the driver's seat.

The man who'd been driven to the precipice would tell you that misfortune had decided his fate once again. The man who has been gifted the chance to view the blackest period of his life from a different perspective would suggest that this act was another cry for help.

When I realised what had happened, I switched off the ignition, removed the hoses and towels, then locked myself in my room. I told no-one. If this was a cry for help, it was a silent one.

CHAPTER **SIXTEEN**

I HAVE no idea what motivated me to keep on living. The days passed in a blur of basic functions: sleep, wake, smoke, shit, smoke, eat, smoke. Repeat. Zippo knocked on my door occasionally to check if I was still alive. A grunt was enough to send him on his way. One or two customers stopped by, angry that I was ignoring their texts and denying them access to Speed Dial's product. I didn't have the energy to face them. Yet deep inside, I must've been clinging to the notion that someone, somewhere, somehow was going to intervene and set my life on a different course. After days of inertia, like a dumb donkey trudging after a carrot, I dragged myself out of bed to attend my next corrections orders appointment, a judicial review of my progress.

I showered, shaved my head, trimmed my goatee, dug out my dishevelled black shirt and suit and asked Zippo for the keys to a Mazda 626 that we used as a pool car for the house. Then I collected my paperwork, which I kept in the bedside drawer, and the remainder of my stash, about a quarter of a bag, or seven grams, which would've disappeared by the time I got back if I'd left it at Zippo's. It was a ten-minute drive to Werribee Magistrates' Court, where a judge would assess whether or not to continue with the corrections orders. In the back of my mind I hoped that an astute judge might see what a mess I was and realise that compulsory rehab was a better option than pointless meetings with overworked and under-equipped counsellors.

As I exited the Princes Highway those dreaded flashing lights appeared in the rear-view mirror. Then the *whoop-whoop* sound that still triggers a nervous twitch to this day. I pulled over, thinking that if I'd been speeding or had jumped a red light I might escape with a spot fine. But in the wing mirror I could see that this officer oozed intent, striding towards my car like John Wayne.

'Name,' he demanded, with the personal skills of a scorpion.

'Simon Fenech.'

'Licence.'

'I don't have it on me at the moment. Just nipped out for some shopping.'

His eyes lit up. 'Stay in the car while I radio through.'

Fuck. Just stay calm and he might not find the ice. And the judicial review won't hear about this today. You can figure it out later. The cop ambled back to my car just as an unmarked car pulled up. *Here we go. They know who I am. That's my corrections orders fucked. I'm going to jail.* My instinct was to run and my hand darted towards the ignition. But Officer Wayne was quicker. In a flash he reached in through the window, grabbed the keys and threw them on the ground.

'You're going nowhere, Fenech. You're under arrest for driving while disqualified, so stay nice and calm there. Then we'll see what other little gifts you have for us this morning.'

The procedure was now routine: I was cuffed, driven to the cop shop, processed, had my shoelaces and belt removed, and placed in a holding cell. One of the desk officers took great delight in telling me that the bag of ice had been found, the court had been notified and a warrant had been issued to search Zippo's house. There was more stolen gear there than at a pawn shop. Of much more concern, having breached both corrections orders, was the fact that all my previous offences would now come back into play. Applying for bail would be pointless. *I'm in here for the next five years*, I thought. *And who'll be waiting for me when I'm released? Nobody. I can't face this. I just can't.*

I looked around the cell. There was nothing to hang from, even if I could've made a noose out of my shirt or pants. It would be ages before I was transferred to a holding prison, either the Melbourne Assessment Prison (the MAP) or the dreaded Sub, and only one way I could avoid that fate. My empty meal tray had just been collected, so I wouldn't be checked again for another hour. I had a narrow window in which to act. I took off my shirt and tied the two sleeves around my neck. Then I lay on my back and pulled the knot tight until I could feel my eyes bulging from their sockets. I wedged my hands under my back and promised myself not to loosen the knot. I choked, I writhed, I prayed. *God, if you exist, allow me to pass out before my next breath.*

***

THE KNOT had been tight enough to restrict blood flow to my head, but not to prevent oxygen from reaching my lungs. Even so, my face turned purple and I pissed myself, a side-effect of strangulation. Perhaps I was lucky and coughed loudly or kicked the wall involuntarily. But a desk officer found me and raised the alarm. Yet again I was transferred to Werribee Hospital, where I was kept overnight under guard to check there was no lasting damage. My vocal cords were bruised and I could only croak one-word answers the following day, but my windpipe was intact.

From there I was transferred to the acute mental health unit of the MAP in the CBD and placed on suicide watch. Every precaution was taken to prevent a repeat attempt to neck myself. I wore a paper-thin gown and the finger food was served on cardboard trays with no utensils. The TV, mounted high up on the wall, was protected by a perspex sheet which was so faded and scratched that I could hardly see the screen. In any case, wall-to-wall MTV love songs like Adele's 'Hello' were perhaps not the best medicine. *Hello from the other fucking side, indeed.*

It took four days for the medication to kick in and for the doctors to release me into a shared cell. I could shower again, and feel the sun on my face for an hour a day in the small exercise courtyard. Fighting the withdrawal, I slept and slept. My body craved rest.

After two weeks at the MAP, I was transferred to the maximum security Metropolitan Remand Centre at Ravenhall Prison, where I would stay until my bail hearing. For the first time it felt like I was looking at a significant stretch inside; surely no chance of another bail reprieve. That feeling of dejection alone should be enough of a deterrent to stop anyone from reoffending. Dread invades your every thought. Your life instantly becomes a half-death. And for a father, the shame of being forcefully separated from your children is excruciating. *Never again*, I told myself. *Keep your head down and do your time. But never, ever again put yourself in this position.*

The strip search was thorough compared to the cursory checks at the cop shop and the MAP. Shake your socks and jocks out, open your mouth, check behind your ears, lift your ball sack, bend over and spread your cheeks, raise your feet – the routine was to become second nature. Then the new intake was herded into the 'fishbowl', a circular waiting room with perspex walls covered in spit and scoured with signatures. The screws looked on from the other side while each prisoner saw a shrink and classification officer in one of the side rooms. I was placed in the Billingham unit along with other patients with mental health issues. In the next holding area we surrendered our clothing and belongings except for our jocks, socks and shoes. We were allocated a green tracksuit, shorts, a white T-shirt and a toiletry pack consisting of soap, a toothbrush and a small tube of toothpaste to tide us over until we had enough money to buy our own. Finally came the catwalk – where new prisoners are paraded past the solitary inmates, who scream abuse and bang their meal tins on the bars to welcome their new prey. It was like walking outside a dog run, with rabid animals clawing at the mesh to get at you. It's impossible not to be intimidated.

The place was feral. Most inmates were coming down from drugs and their fuses were further shortened by the insecurity of being on remand. Tensions were higher than ever following a riot just a few months earlier, when four hundred prisoners went apeshit the day before a state-wide smoking ban was introduced, attacking guards with rocks and teargas, lighting fires and ramming the gates with commandeered vehicles. The damage, caused over fifteen hours before crack response teams regained control, cost the state more than $10 million. All prisoners were now on 23-hour lockdown until the prison was refurbished. During the short exercise break the only connection with the outside world was the sound of rush-hour traffic from the nearby freeways. On tip-toes, from one corner of the exercise area, the top of one tree could be glimpsed above the imposing concrete wall.

Code alarms, activated when a prisoner received a flogging from other inmates, were constant. Every night the corridors echoed with threats and insults. My nerves were frazzled. Just two or three cells away one prisoner 'bronzed-up', covering himself in his own shit in protest at delays to his bail hearing. I was barely aware of the other guys in my cell, who regularly chopped and changed. Instead of engaging with them, I wrapped myself in my blanket, put on two sets of clothes to cope with the cold draughts, and curled up into a tight ball on my bunk. I had zero skills to cope with life behind bars and my thoughts rarely ventured beyond self-harm.

During those wretched two weeks before my bail hearing, an unlikely ally was beavering away behind the scenes to get me out. I'd been calling Michelle regularly and, not wanting Brodie's dad to spend his formative years behind bars, she sold my GT ute to pay for Patrick Casey to try to work his magic yet again. With forty years' experience in the courts, Patrick knew all the judges and prosecutors. His best work was carried out behind closed doors and he was often sure of the result well before the actual court hearing. But not this time. Even he was worried.

'Prepare for the worst,' he said. 'I've pulled out all the stops. She could go either way. It's all down to you now.'

In the past I'd played the part of the repentant sinner to a tee. All those hours watching *Judge Judy* and other courtroom dramas paid off. This time my performance was genuine. I couldn't face being sent back inside. I begged for one last chance, for an opportunity to start afresh. And I cried with a conviction that no Hollywood actor could've faked. When the judge announced that, considering my mental health history, she was willing to try CISP bail one final time, I dropped to my knees in the dock.

The thud of the gavel was as resounding as my determination that, from that day in late November 2015 on, I would stay clean and out of trouble.

***

MICHELLE HAD shown how much she cared by paying for Patrick and it seemed only right to give things another go, at the very least for Brodie's sake. He was the focus of my attempts to turn over a new leaf. I wasn't going to even attempt to reconnect with Jake and Mackenzie until I could trust myself. I stayed at Michelle's house for a few nights but the truce was soon shattered. My emotional resilience was too fragile for confrontation and it became clear that Michelle and I could only ever function as co-parents, not partners. I visited Vic, and started the long process of becoming a prodigal brother, but he couldn't let me stay again, and I understood that.

My only option was to skulk back to Zippo's, the worst place possible for a recovering addict. I expected resentment that my arrest had triggered the raid. Instead, the others kept out of my way, no doubt guilty that most of my belongings which hadn't been seized by the cops were long gone. But I didn't want to lock myself away in my room again. Isolation was the enemy, giving me too much time for self-pity, which always led to ice. So I forced myself to socialise and that meant hanging around these big-time users, watching their puff haze thicken. Someone had tracked down Speed Dial, which I was glad about because the pressure was off me to deal. Several times a day I was offered a pipe, but I refused every time. There's a saying that 'if you sit in the barber's chair for long enough, you'll eventually get a haircut'. Not me. My resolve was ironclad. Watching those blokes smoke themselves into oblivion disgusted me. There was no way I was going back to that living hell and no way I was going back to prison.

If I'd needed any extra incentive to stay clean, January provided all the proof necessary that ice use never ends well. I attended no fewer than five funerals, all of former addicts. First to go was Bluey, the White Gorilla, who died of emphysema and heart issues at the age of fifty-four. He'd had my back, despite all the shit with the bent copper Jack Bennett, and I was proud to carry his coffin. Next was Hunter, a major dealer, who was having problems with one of the Asian cartels who owed him $25,000. He died of a heroin overdose but he was way too smart for that. The word on the street was that the cartel hit him with a 'hot shot'. Sharky, a regular customer, was killed on his way to work when a car T-boned his motorbike. Jacko, another meth addict, died while blowing a glass pipe in his garage when the gas cylinder exploded. And finally Hodgy, a bloke I knew from my trucking days, died of a heart attack. The same haunted faces appeared at every funeral and then disappeared, undeterred, to continue to dig their own graves.

To provide some release from the darkness I got a bunch more tatts from a big Maori guy who was a regular at Zippo's. The designs were a psychologist's dream – all dark, angry and dangerous. The date of baby Charlie's birth was an obvious addition. He inked the word RESPECT across my chest. What or whom I respected was unclear. FENECH was emblazoned across the small of my back in big, bold, angry letters. There were playing cards, a revolver, the cross of Jesus, and many skulls, including one in the middle of a huge Maltese cross on my back. After a three-day bender, the Maori then attempted my family tree on the left side of my chest, but fucked it up by writing 'Daff' instead of 'Dave' and had to draw a real tree instead. I got him to cover Kylie's name with a sad clown face. Three wise monkeys, who could see no evil, speak no evil and hear no evil, looked pure evil. My skin was a blueprint of a life gone wrong and a constant reminder of what I wanted to leave behind.

I fulfilled all my CISP obligations, regularly taking the bus-train-tram to the other side of Melbourne, often with barely enough money for the return fares. And then, on 4 February 2016, just over two months since I was released on bail, I screwed up. Yes, I was depressed. Yes, coming off a $1000-a-day habit was excruciating. Yes, I was struggling for money. But why the fuck did I take the new pool car at Zippo's, a Holden Astra, and drive to a counselling appointment just a few kilometres away? I could have walked. I could have crawled. But no. I was beating my ice addiction, but I just couldn't break the habit of driving unlicensed. So there's no defence. I wasn't asking for trouble, I was demanding it.

The Astra's rego had elapsed by just one day. The automatic number plate recognition software in a patrol car pinged me immediately. When the lights flashed and the siren sounded, I pulled over and slumped over the steering wheel. All roads led back to prison. The officer walked over and I wound the window down, ready to beg him to turn a blind eye. But when he asked to see my licence something snapped. I just couldn't face going back behind bars. This officer was way more casual than the previous one, more concerned with putting on a show for the rubber-necking public than paying proper attention to me. So I seized my chance to start the engine and I floored the Astra, all 1.6 litres of it, leaving the cop gawping in amazement.

My advantage lasted for about a minute before I saw the tell-tale lights in the rear-view mirror. My only hope was to out-fox them. A red light at the busy intersection ahead might be my chance. One car was waiting to turn right and another, coming from the other direction, was also edging across the junction. I clipped the rear of the car on my side and bounced off the front of the second car but made it through. Glancing in the mirror I saw that those two cars had blocked the junction, preventing the coppers from following. The relief was short-lived; I heard a chopper circling overhead. I'd seen enough episodes of *Highway Patrol* to know that I had to head for a residential area to try to shake them, so I swerved hard right onto a side road. Too hard. The front wheels locked, the back end skidded around and the passenger side of the Astra wrapped itself neatly around a gum tree.

In a blind panic I leapt out of the car and started running down another side street before realising I'd left my phone and laptop behind, both of which would identify me. Already blowing out my arse, I jogged back to the car and grabbed them. A crowd had gathered.

'Don't worry, it's all good. It's my car, not stolen,' I panted, and set off again. Whenever there was a side street I took it, but the chopper seemed to track my every move. I was running out of breath, but the fear of returning to jail drove me forward. Then, just in the nick of time, a stroke of luck. A white car with real estate agent branding on the side turned into the street that I was halfway along and slowed down behind me.

Thank fuck for that, he's going to offer me a lift, I thought. And I was partly correct because, grinning out of the passenger window, was the cop who had pulled me over. His partner swerved onto the footpath to block my escape but my legs had already surrendered. I tried one last side-step but the grinning cop jumped out and tackled me around the waist. His partner stopped the car and joined in, driving a knee into my back and smashing my face into the road. One of my top front teeth was knocked out and three others split in half.

'I'm clean, I'm clean!' I spluttered through a mouthful of blood.

'Bit late to tell us that now,' said the copper, cuffing my hands behind my back. 'Why did you run? We only stopped you for driving an unregistered car. Now you're in a world of shit.'

CHAPTER **SEVENTEEN**

THE EXPRESSION on the smirking female copper's face at my bail hearing at Sunshine Magistrates' Court said it all – *gotcha*. The police left nothing to chance and I was whisked straight in front of the judge at the courthouse so that I didn't see a bail justice, who were often more lenient. Even my barrister had given up on me. He went through the motions of applying for bail with about as much conviction as if he were defending OJ Simpson. The judge, with Brylcreemed hair and the posture of a meerkat, wasn't having a bar of it.

'Mr Fenech, I find this bail application insulting. Time and again my colleagues have given you a chance and time and again you spat that chance back in their faces. Your previous convictions indicate a man who has total contempt for the law. And your argument that driving without a licence is a victimless crime displays a reckless arrogance. The laws of our roads are there to protect the public. By once again trying to evade the police in a high-speed chase you have provided further evidence that you are a danger not only to yourself but to all those around you. It's a miracle that the only injuries sustained were to your own face.'

'But that was when the coppers . . .' I tried to explain.

'Quiet, Fenech. This court's patience is exhausted. Your mitigation that you have been clean of drugs for two months carries no substance. Perhaps you should have tried that years ago. You will be remanded in custody until your sentencing. Take him out of my sight.'

And so, just weeks after I promised myself that I would never return to prison, I was back at the Metropolitan Remand Centre. If possible, I felt more dejected than when I arrived the first time. On one hand, I had no chance of any reprieve because I was now facing a new charge of reckless driving endangering life, which carried a maximum penalty of ten years. So the MRC was likely to be home for some time. But on the other hand, I hadn't touched ice in two months. My body was starting to mend, although my head needed more time to fully recover. Sleep had cushioned my previous stint in the MRC, but the 23-hour lockdown regime would now be tougher. I had to devise a strategy for survival and it hinged on two things: lying low and retaining respect.

I'd learnt a lot from the Sylvester Stallone movie *Lock Up*. Stallone's character, Frank Leone, had one motto – don't trust anyone – or DTA. It worked fine till he got on the wrong side of the warden just before he was due to be released and ended up serving many additional years. Make the wrong moves inside prison and a two-year stretch can turn into life, so I was determined to keep my head down. But it's a delicate line to tread. You have to stand up for yourself, for your own safety, but also to avoid the various gangs who are all too ready to take advantage of you. I wasn't going to be the mug who cleaned everyone else's trainers, gave up their food, or dished out blowjobs in the showers.

The first test came from my cellmate, a cocky Italian kid in his twenties, with a pock-marked face and a physique carved out of Roman marble. His name was Rocky, funnily enough. At first we were respectful towards each other, especially over when to shit. We agreed that we'd do everything possible to hold it in until our one hour of exercise time and then use the brasco in our cell while the other was out. (I had no idea what a brasco was until a few days into my first MRC stint a bloke told me he was going to 'the brasco' and I asked if I'd join him. That kind of naivety can be dangerous!) Our shitting regime worked well for a while and, despite the 23-hour lockdown, we managed to put up with each other without ever being mates or coming to blows. That's a feat in itself. But as young Rocky got settled, his confidence grew, and he began strutting around with his sunnies on his head like he owned the fucking joint. Soon enough, he was making connections with influential prisoners and mouthing off to other inmates and the screws. Then, one afternoon without warning, he decided to curl one out in our cell just before mealtime.

'What the fuck, man?' I spluttered when the first waft woke me up. 'Why didn't you go during exercise? That's putrid.'

'Fuck that, man. I don't get enough exercise time. Got to look after these bad boys.' He smirked and kissed his biceps. 'Just get used to it, okay?'

He had crossed a line and the atmosphere between us instantly turned sour. It worsened when we lost our TV privileges for a week when he got lippy with a screw. A couple of days later I spotted him pointing me out to a few other prisoners as I did laps of the yard. At the end of the exercise hour we returned to our cell.

'Talking about me out there, were you?' I asked him.

'Not you, your runners. Actually, my runners. I'm taking them.'

'The fuck you talking about?'

'Decent runners. Nikes'll fetch a lot in here. You'll find another pair –' Rocky had just about uttered the word 'soon' when my hand clamped round his throat and pinned him against the wall.

'Now listen here, you little fuck,' I growled. 'You have two days to transfer the fuck out of this cell. Make up some excuse that doesn't get me in trouble. And tell your mates that if any of those pricks so much as catch my eye again, they'll need more than a good pair of runners.' And that was the end of Rocky, who disappeared from my prison life like a neatly flushed turd.

His gang didn't bother me again, either, but that wasn't my only problem in those early weeks, when every new inmate is potential prey. The prison was full of addicts that I used to deal to. Every one of them owed me money and it was tempting to lean on them to pay me back, because inside prison the value of everything is magnified. Even a teaspoon of sugar was a bargaining tool. But a stint in the slot – solitary confinement – for punching someone out wasn't worth the risk.

Soon after Rocky left, I found out one of my former customers had been bad-mouthing me, or 'air-raiding' as it's known inside, telling anyone who'd listen that I'd done a run-through on his ex-girlfriend's place to chase a bad debt. It was total bullshit.

I didn't know his ex-girlfriend and chasing debts like that was never my style. Going after a sheila would have been looked down on inside, especially among the bikies. I didn't want my stay to be a series of confrontations. It was time to send out a message – don't fuck with me.

I watched this crumb like a hawk during exercise time over a number of days to see if he was mixing with anyone I should be worried about. But he mainly hung around other junkies. On the way back from the yard one day, I followed his cellmate and, just before he reached their cell, tapped him on the shoulder and told him to make himself scarce for five minutes. He was staunch, meaning he would keep quiet, because snitching was as good as admitting yourself to the infirmary. When the corridor was quiet, I slipped into their cell and closed the door. The cameras would have picked me up entering and leaving, but I left no other visible trace. The prick struggled to breathe for a few weeks. That was the first and last time he bad-mouthed me. The word 'respect' travels fast in jail, and nobody looked to pick a fight with me again.

***

ON 23-HOUR lockdown, you take every opportunity to get out of your cell. I desperately wanted a job to keep myself occupied but also so I could earn some money. No-one else was going to top up my account with the $120 maximum allowed each month. I couldn't even afford extra underwear and had to wash my one pair of socks and a pair of jocks by hand each day. Better that than losing them in the prison laundry. I needed money for phone calls, too, and had to find a new lawyer after I sacked Patrick. I craved luxuries like some extra 2 Minute Noodles or a packet of chips or some tropical flavour cordial to supplement the basic rations. And the food really was basic. The butter chicken was chicken-free and if you found a cube of beef in your stroganoff you thought you'd won the lottery. Instead of protein we were loaded up with starchy carbs like rice, pasta, potatoes and bread.

I applied for a job in the kitchens, but this was before I'd gained everyone's respect and the thought of having a pot of boiling water 'accidentally' spilt over me didn't appeal. Then a position in the metal shop came up, learning how to weld. The tooling was actually quite sophisticated and we made everything from prison bunks, chairs and tables, to farm gates. It kept me out of the cell from 8 a.m. to 3 p.m. and earnt me a whole $32 per week. Apart from the money, I was wearing overalls and safety boots again, working as part of a team and acquiring new skills. I felt a new purpose and the screws in the metal shop were half-decent, trying to help rather than punish. The inmates on the welding course had a different attitude, too. These blokes wanted to put their pasts behind them and do something with their lives.

One bloke was a career criminal who only worked one night of the year. He would stake out a wealthy Chinese family for months and then clean them out when they left home to celebrate Chinese New Year. I called him the Pink Panther, after the cat burglar that Inspector Clouseau could never catch. Except my Pink Panther was obviously not that good! An older guy, Pops, was a country farmer who lost the plot in a dispute over a dirt track and shot a neighbour and his parents. Another family man, in his mid-thirties, hit and killed a pedestrian while driving off his face on xanny, the highly addictive benzo, Xanax. Timmy, a former meth addict whose wife was gang-raped when she went to collect some gear for him, half-killed one of the men with a claw-hammer. Countless blokes had breached their AVOs. Others simply owed thousands in fines. Was prison really the best place for people who couldn't afford to pay trumped-up penalties? Some brought their troubles on themselves, many more didn't. In all these people there was a common denominator – prison could so easily have been avoided. And every morning I spoke two words to myself, over and over, to sear the message into my brain: *Fuck jail, fuck jail, fuck jail, fuck jail, fuck jail* . . .

Gradually, my mind started to clear. The first sign of this was the return of dreams, more than four months after my last ice use. In the grip of addiction, the brain cannot properly reabsorb dopamine and serotonin, both of which contribute to the deep stage of sleep called REM, or rapid eye movement. That's when a person dreams. My first dream in years completely freaked me out because it felt so real! The bloke in the next cell heard me yelling out 'stop it' and giggling uncontrollably, because as far as I was concerned, Jake was chasing me around the backyard with a water pistol. It said a lot about the emotions I'd buried that my kids were first to reach the surface of my recovering subconscious.

As mental clarity continued to return, I was able to start piecing together the previous few years. It wasn't a pretty picture and I initially obsessed over details. Charlie's grave still didn't have a headstone. I hadn't attended the wakes of my brother and mum. I'd argued with my brother over money shortly before his death. The fact that I had no photos of my kids or other members of the family on my cell wall destroyed me at first. But it gradually made me realise how much I missed those stable days, when my home, my family and my toys were everything a man could've asked for. This epiphany helped me to turn regret into a motivation. Sure, I'd been dealt some bum cards. The horrified reaction from other participants in group counselling sessions was proof that my story was remarkable, even for prison. Guys, most of whom had endured their own share of misery, went out of their way to congratulate me on my survival.

But I hadn't played the cards that had been dealt me well. I had to accept responsibility for my own failings and ditch the self-pity. It was time to stop dwelling on what I'd lost and focus on what I had left – three beautiful children and a loving brother. This was more than many people had. What was to stop me from building a new life, maybe out in the country away from the temptations and pressures of the city, and achieving that happiness again? I'd be starting from rock bottom and there'd be challenges, but I started to dream again during waking hours, too, and imagined a road map back to normality with small, achievable stepping stones of ambition.

Vic's visits every second Wednesday were a mixed blessing. Of course I was happy to see him, albeit ashamed of my circumstances. But it was also a major pain in the arse to go through screening and strip searches before and after each visit. We were forced to wear a one-piece monkey suit that zipped up the back and was cable-tied behind the neck so that nothing could be smuggled in or out. For the first couple of months I just offloaded my anger and frustrations on Vic. *Had he chased that money that was owed to me? Was my Harley missing from Zippo's? Where were we at with finding a solicitor for my sentencing?* He sat patiently listening to my rants, nodding occasionally but unwilling to act as my messenger in the outside world.

And then one Wednesday his eyes lit up. 'You're different today, brother,' he said. 'None of the negative stuff. You look a lot better, too. Calmer.'

'It's coming off the drugs. I'm only just starting to fully recover, you know. I honestly believe I've turned the corner. God's on my side again, too.' I gave him a big grin.

I'd been enrolling for every available course – dealing with worry and emotions, parenting, drug counselling, driving awareness, dealing with loss, forensic mental health – and badgering the decent screws to consider me as a stand-in for some courses with seven-month waiting lists. My way hadn't been working on the outside and I was determined to equip myself with every possible tool for coping with life again. These courses were my rehab and, as part of that journey, I made an appointment to see the prison chaplain. She was a lovely, scatty lady, with tousled grey hair and a wonderfully kind face. Two sentences into my life story and I was crying buckets. The chaplain smiled softly, took my hands in hers and joined me in tears. It was my first meaningful human contact in years. It might sound clichéd but I felt a spiritual presence re-enter my body and a light and warmth fill the soulless void that I'd been carrying around. Had God decided that my divine punishment was over and that it was time for me to earn redemption? I was ready to welcome Him back into my life, that's for sure. I read the passages of the Bible that the chaplain pointed me towards, I started attending Mass every Sunday and even joined in singing the hymns. Just my luck, the first hymn we sang was 'Amazing Grace'. Okay, I'm no Pavarotti but I belted the first verse out with all my heart.

Amazing Grace! How sweet the sound; That saved a wretch like me! I once was lost, but now am found; Was blind, but now I see.

I blubbed my way through the rest of the hymn. It felt like the words had been written just for me.

***

TIMMY'S EYES lit up when I told him I'd been given a new Bible. Like me, he was coming off a serious meth addiction and, also like me, was finding that nicotine withdrawal was almost as tough. Even though cigarettes had been banned the previous year, leading to those riots at the MRC, tobacco still made its way inside, usually via the screws, and was just about the most valuable commodity. One fifty-gram pouch would cost $1300 and the money had to be deposited into an outside bank account up front. One pre-made ciggie, containing just a shred of tobacco, cost $20. The nicotine hit was negligible.

'If you think you're using pages from my Bible for roll-ups, you've got another thing coming,' I told Timmy. 'There's no way I'm crossing God again. Anyway, how did you get hold of some baccie?'

'It's not for tobacco. I know another way of getting a nicotine hit. And don't freak out, we can use the waxy wrapping paper from toilet rolls instead of Bible pages.' Timmy then proceeded to walk me through the 25-step, sixteen-hour manufacturing process to make one DIY tobacco ciggie using nicotine patches (which were standard issue to all heavy smokers) and teabags.

It was such a long process that it was impossible to hide it from the screws. They soon realised how the toilet roll wrappers were being used and removed the packaging. That's when the Bible became very popular.

They were also good at spotting the tiniest remnants of ash, or finding where we hid the ciggies by using the milk bottle label to stick them under a table or chair. The punishment was to take the kettle away, so we had to find a new way of lighting the ciggie. This was equally inventive. The foil cover of a jar of coffee was removed, torn in two and each half folded many times to make two separate prongs. The end of each prong was then bent at an angle, one a little further than the other. Next some shampoo or body wash was placed in plastic spoon, with toilet paper at the ready. The prongs were poked into the top two slots of a power socket and the bent end of one dipped in the shampoo. Then the power switch was flicked on and the spoon tilted so that the end of the other prong briefly dipped in the shampoo, which acted as a conductor and created a few sparks to set the toilet paper alight. That was the theory, anyway. The first time Timmy and I tried this we dipped both prongs in the shampoo before switching on the power and shorted the whole landing, on a Saturday night when everyone wanted to watch footy. It just goes to show – there's no such thing as a victimless crime!

***

AS THE day of my sentencing approached, I couldn't stop myself from hoping. Maybe, just maybe, my record of good behaviour and the self-improvement programs that I'd attended would convince the judge to let me off with time served, about four months at that point. I had a new solicitor on my side, a thorough professional called Sandra Gaunt, who came recommended to me by the Pink Panther. To make sure she had all the facts at her disposal I wrote down my life history on eighteen pages of A4 paper. Vic again forked out for a new barrister, a bloke named Geoffrey Harrison, who was caked in fake tan, stank of cigarettes and looked as though he'd come straight off the set of *Law & Order*. I promised to pay Vic back by selling off the stock of parts that I'd been storing on the farm in Melton.

'Your Honour, we are here today to talk about the rise, and fall, and rise again of Simon Fenech,' Geoffrey bellowed after the prosecution had argued for ninety minutes that I should be locked up forever and a day. The judge, a petite lady in her sixties, hung on his every word and was showing promising signs of empathy, especially when Geoffrey read dramatically from my potted history. My hopes of imminent freedom were rising.

'Mr Fenech, this is all too much to take in,' said the judge. 'I need to take your files away and study them again in more detail.' I could picture her reading my case documents at home in her favourite armchair, Siamese cat in her lap and a glass of sherry in her hand. 'This case will be adjourned for one month.'

A month? How much sherry did she need? I was shattered. Every diabolical aspect of the MRC – spreading my arse cheeks at the screening, the slop served for dinner, the constant screams of abuse – was accentuated on my return. *One more month*, I told myself, *you can do it.*

Or it would have been a month, if the bus had showed up to take a group of us to court on my appointed day. But someone simply forgot to book it! So after having been woken at 4 a.m. and subjected to the humiliation of a strip search, we all had to be searched again before returning to our cells. Then, two weeks later, I went through the same ritual and spent the whole morning in the court's holding cell, chewing my nails to the quick and frustrated that Vic would be there waiting patiently on his own. Some of the group returned, raging that their sentences were harsher than expected. Others were obviously released. *Please let that be me*, I thought.

Finally my name was called and I was cuffed to be taken up in the elevator to the waiting area outside court, only to be told that the previous case had overrun and the judge had called a recess for lunch. So it was back down in the lift to hang around for another hour. My nerves were shredded. Then, after hearing the same arguments from the same people, the judge still couldn't make up her mind and adjourned for another three weeks. The charm of this old lady was wearing thin and those extra twenty-one days seemed like an eternity. Every morning I crossed off another day on my calendar which featured a picture of a painting called *The Annunciation* showing the Angel Gabriel appearing to the Virgin Mary. It was stuck to my cell wall with toothpaste, right next to my picture of Marilyn Monroe. But, unlike nearly every straight guy in the prison, I didn't crave the touch of a woman. The thought of holding Brodie in my arms again was all the motivation I needed to endure the last stretch.

On the day of the final hearing I said my goodbyes to Pops, Pink Panther, Dizzy and a couple of the decent screws. Vic was waiting in court, as always, and showed me his crossed fingers as I was led into the room. The judge walked in and I detected the faintest of smiles as she glanced my way.

'Thank you for your patience in this matter, Mr Fenech. This has been a particularly difficult case for me and I have been searching for the fairest way forward. The loss of one family member can be enough to send someone off the rails. For you to lose several close family members in such a short space of time, and then to lose an infant daughter, created an incredible emotional burden. And the court is mindful of the efforts that you have recently shown to address your drug addiction and to turn your life around.

'I was also appreciative of the personal letter you wrote to me, explaining the depth of your remorse and your plans for a new life. However, several of your charges carry a mandatory prison sentence, which is something I cannot ignore. Taking into account the time you have spent at the MRC and the exceptional burden of the 23-hour lockdown, I sentence you to another six months in prison, on top of your five months already served on remand. On release you will be subject to an eighteen-month Community Corrections Order, three hundred and eighty hours of community service, drug and alcohol counselling, mental health counselling; you must complete a drug driving course before you are eligible for a new licence, and a men's behaviour change program. I wish you well in your recovery.'

What just happened? I thought I was getting out today. Another six fucking months? No. No. No. I swivelled round in the dock to look at Vic, a little too sharply for the liking of the dock officers, who tensed. Vic's faced contorted in pain and he clasped his hands. He knew that my resolve to start afresh was strong, but he probably doubted my resilience. My solicitor, Sandra, approached the dock.

'Can we appeal?' I asked in desperation.

'You'll be out before any appeal is heard,' she said. 'And besides, it's probably a fair judgement. Honestly, I thought it would be much longer.'

As the officers led me away, I glanced back at Vic and mouthed 'thanks', knowing I wouldn't be seeing him for a while. My next destination was anyone's guess. From the court I'd be taken back to the sentence management unit at MRC, from where I'd be transferred to a medium security jail as a medium B category prisoner. I was praying that it wouldn't be Port Phillip, better known as Port Putrid, an old, ugly and decrepit jail near Laverton North, way too close to my old associates. Marngoneet, near Geelong, was known for a program-based approach to reintegration and would've been my preference.

But it was to be neither. The following day I received the news that I was going to Fulham Correctional Centre in Gippsland, a three-hour drive from Melbourne. Using my last call from the MRC, I insisted to Vic that it was too far to drive for the one-hour visits. 'Look, brother, it is what it is. You'll be doing me a favour by staying away. Six months will fly by if I'm cut off from the outside world.' I was doing my best to disguise my utter dejection. 'It can't be any worse than the MRC. I'll just keep my head down and do the time. The best thing about Fulham is that I won't know anyone in there and won't be hassled.'

How wrong I was . . .

CHAPTER **EIGHTEEN**

THE DOOR to my room in the lodge I shared with eight other inmates burst open and in barged Razor, the top dog of one of the bikie gangs, a snarling human pit bull with a formidable Mohican. My heart sank. A visit from Razor always spelt trouble.

Since arriving at Fulham I'd kept my nose clean and stayed out of the disputes between the different gangs: bikies, Pacific Islanders or the Aboriginal inmates. Lockdowns, when tensions spiralled out of control, were frequent. But in other ways Fulham was like a breath of fresh air compared to the MRC. Out my window I could see the lush Gippsland farmland, rolling hills and an endless expanse of blue sky that whispered freedom. The wind on my face in the exercise paddock was a sensory overload. Dopamine had returned to my system and at long last I could feel pleasure again. Eager to keep occupied, I quickly secured a job in the run-down metal shop. It was situated in an old aerodrome and we serviced the prison's lawnmowers, the quadbikes that pulled food trolleys and the golf buggy 'ambulance'. Inmates also made spit roasts from hot water tanks or potbelly stoves from truck wheel hubs. Working in the metal shop was a privilege, especially when the alternative was getting infected by the macho bullshit in the gym.

The rooms in each lodge held one inmate, with a communal kitchen, dining area, laundry and lounge. My fellow lodgers were tolerable once I'd laid down a few ground rules about noise and respecting my space. It helped that a bloke in another part of the prison had been a decent kickboxer, so my reputation spread quickly. I became a sort of father figure, often cooking fried chicken or lasagne for the whole lodge. I didn't want to be Mr Popular, I just wanted to do my time without aggravation. But no-one escapes being inside without paying some kind of dues. And Razor clearly hadn't interrupted my precious downtime to chat about the price of fish.

He strode over to my table, sat down and fixed me with a stare that could've frozen the fires of Hell. 'Fenech! I heard about you,' he said, with soft menace behind his rasping voice. 'How's that young boy of yours doing?'

'Is there something you need?' I said, putting my book down and sitting up on the edge of my bed. I wanted him to see that I wasn't scared, but the truth was I'd been dreading this moment ever since my first arrest – the safety of my loved ones was back on the line.

'How did you guess? But no need to be shitty about it. Do us a solid and we'll leave you alone. If you don't, then we have a problem.'

'Go ahead.'

'You work in G Block, don't you?'

'Yeah . . .'

'We need you to make a shiv. There's a war brewing and we need to show them who's who in the zoo.'

'Come on, man. I've only got a few months left. Can't one of your other soldiers do it?'

'We like to share this stuff round. Avoids suspicion. Your boy's called Brodie, right?'

I was caught between a rock and a hard place. If I made the shiv I risked losing my privileges; I could even get extra jail time. And of course some poor bastard was going to bleed like a stuck pig. But if I refused, I'd be worried sick about what might be happening on the outside.

'How the fuck am I supposed to smuggle a shiv out through the metal detector?' I asked.

Turned out Razor had it all planned, right down to the exact size of steel offcut he wanted. Making the blade on one of the metal grinders without being noticed would be the hardest part. Then I had to drop it in a certain bin in the metal room at the end of the shift and another of Razor's associates would pick it up the following morning when the bins were emptied.

I had a narrow window for pulling this off and was a bucket of nerves. Make the shiv too early and the chances of it being discovered in the bin were higher. Leave it too late and I might miss an opportunity when the guards were distracted. Fortunately, I found a short piece of flat plate steel in the scrap bucket and it only took me a few minutes to sharpen it behind one of the welder's screens. I stuck it down my sock which was hidden by my trackie bottoms and walked like a penguin for the rest of the afternoon. Five minutes before the end of the shift I transferred the blade up my sleeve, collected a small waste bin from the lunchroom and emptied the contents, including the shiv, into the designated wheelie bin. I'd kept my side of the bargain. Now all I could do was hope that my handiwork might never be put to use.

Stabbings were not uncommon at Fulham. Shortly before I got there, an inmate had been stabbed multiple times with a sharpened toothbrush over a $20 cigarette debt. There was actually more chance of a stabbing going undetected than some of the brutal beatings, which were constant. Thankfully, on this occasion, the screws must've been tipped off about the trouble that was brewing. Two days after I did Razor the favour a full search of the prison was ordered and five other shivs were found in the cells of gang members. They were all sent to solitary and then shipped off to other jails. A bloodbath was avoided but during the search something even deadlier had been discovered. One inmate had caught a baby brown snake, one of the most venomous species in Australia, in the exercise paddock and somehow managed to keep it alive under his bed in a plastic container. Had it not been found, there's no doubt it would have ended up in someone's bed to settle a score.

***

JUST LIKE in the MRC, everything had a value. I continued to make and trade my teabaccy ciggies, but the most valuable commodities were drugs, both medicinal and illicit. And, because prisoners stayed at Fulham a lot longer than at the MRC, much more resourceful methods of supply had evolved. The most valuable drug of all was bupe or chicken (rhyming slang for chicken soup), the street names for buprenorphine, a methadone-like drug used to treat addiction to opioids such as heroin. It was easy to smuggle thin packets of bupe into the prison which would then be divided up and sold for $20 a hit. If you could supply bupe then you lived like a king, even if you happened to be a sex offender or a toucher.

One inmate in our lodge was on methadone and often had to queue for two hours for his meds. After swallowing the syrup in front of the guards and waiting for thirty minutes until he was released, he went straight to his room and vomited into his flimsy cotton underwear to strain his stomach contents. He then sold the filtered liquid for another junkie to inject. Is it possible to stoop any lower?

Others were expert at hiding tablets under their tongues then spitting them out. Anti-depressants changed hands for big dollars. In the area set aside for serial violent offenders (SVOs), the inmates made a makeshift syringe out of a ball-point pen which they shared to inject heroin whenever it was successfully smuggled inside. One SVO's arm became so badly infected it swelled to the size of a melon.

Ice was in ready supply. In my first two weeks at Fulham I shared a cell with an addict in his mid-twenties. He'd been convicted of burglary and managed to smuggle in a bag up his arse. This practice was known as 'shelving'. As soon as the first of the day's four musters was over, his mate snuck in and the pair smoked the ice off a piece of kitchen foil. Even though my addition to ice had been all-consuming, I wanted none of it. All around me people were desperate for anything that could release them from the reality of their sentences or their dependencies. It was horrible to watch and only strengthened my resolve to leave that life behind the second I got out.

Every waking thought was channelled towards the hope of a new start. I spent hours at the wire fence, breathing in the countryside. It reminded me of those two escapes to Mildura. What was to stop me from leaving the city and recreating the simple, nourishing family harmony that I'd so recklessly tossed away? I was leaving nothing to chance and again attended every course possible – relationships, parenting, maths and basic computer skills – anything that would improve the likelihood of survival on the outside.

Nevertheless, leaving prison would be a huge leap into the unknown. I had no money and nowhere to stay. Although I would be technically homeless and therefore a priority, the waiting list for public housing was seven years. Eventually, as my release date approached, and after a lot of gnashing of teeth, I was allocated a room in a boarding house until I made other arrangements. I'd had no contact with Michelle or Brodie, but the girlfriend of another inmate had bumped into them and told me that Brodie was my spitting image. How I missed the little bugger. I wrote regular letters to Jake and Mackenzie. It broke my heart that the letters went unanswered, but I understood. The time for healing would come. Until then, I continued crossing the days off the calendar.

***

AS THE countdown continued, time really started to drag. I'd had a scare a couple of months earlier when the authorities realised that I'd not been sentenced for breaching my previous two corrections orders. I had to plead my case again before a telecourt judge via video link. He was happy to suspend further sentencing until after an assessment of how I was tackling my new corrections orders. There was a downside to this because with outstanding charges hanging over me, I was ineligible for downgrading to a category C prisoner. This prevented me moving to one of the more independent four-bedroom lodges or working outside the jail on the prison farm. But, with freedom within touching distance, it wasn't the time to kick up a fuss.

My final night in Fulham lasted an eternity. The other fellas seemed to snore louder than ever before, like a bunch of geese with bronchitis. I was as nervous as my first day of school and couldn't sleep for running through all my preparations and expectations. Thankfully, those fretful hours were cut short because all five prisoners due for release were woken at 4 a.m. to be processed and subjected to one final degrading spread of the arse cheeks.

The clothes I'd been arrested in were either torn or covered in blood, so I left Fulham wearing a pair of trackies and a hoodie provided by the Salvation Army. My worldly possessions were a small backpack containing certificates from every course I'd completed, my toothbrush, a myki public transport card, and an ATM card containing the $140 I'd saved, plus two weeks of crisis dole, about $300 in total. As the huge prison gates clanked open, I took a few delicious but tentative steps towards the waiting bus, anxiously checking that no coppers were waiting to rearrest me on some trumped-up new charge. The coast was clear. *You can wipe prisoner CRN2068492 off your records*, I said to myself when the gates shut behind me. *He ain't coming back.*

The bus dropped us at Sale train station with just enough time to buy a ticket to Flinders Street in Melbourne's CBD and find a discarded ciggie butt. One of the other men had a lighter and the first drag blew our heads off. It was like smoking for the very first time. When the train arrived, although it was half-empty, the other ex-cons all followed me into the same carriage, which was irritating. I couldn't wait to be away from the constant stream of bullshit I'd endured for the past eight months. One or two were already bragging about their first score or their next scam. *Two more hours and then you're free*, I told myself.

The noise and bustle of Flinders Street was a shock to my system. I'd been conditioned to routine and restriction. After changing to the Werribee line I arrived at the station and called Vic from a public phone. I told him that I was heading to Michelle's to surprise her and Brodie and asked if he'd be able to take me to my boarding house later in the afternoon.

'It's great to hear you so upbeat, brother,' Vic said. 'But just remember that everyone else has been getting on with their lives without you. Don't expect too much.' Werribee was no different, though. The first two people I passed as I walked to Michelle's place were old ice customers, minus a few teeth but still hanging to score some gear.

Michelle opened her front door and stared at me.

'Just got out this morning,' I said with a beaming smile.

'Just got out of where? Who are you? Fuck! Simon, I honestly didn't recognise you. You look so healthy.'

Prison food wasn't great, but I'd probably consumed more

calories in the previous eight months than my whole seven years of ice addiction. I'd piled on about twenty kilos.

'Is Brodie here? I'm desperate to see him.'

'No, he's at childcare. I'll be picking him up in an hour or so. I suppose you could come along. But you can't wait here. I've got, er, company. Please don't make a scene.'

'Whoa! That's not me anymore. I'm clean now.' I ignored the roll of her eyes. 'Look, I'll make myself scarce and be back in an hour.'

Brodie spotted his mum as soon as we arrived at the childcare centre and came running. She picked him up and said, 'Look who's here. It's Dad.' Brodie buried his head in her bosom. 'He was only fifteen months old when you went away. He probably doesn't remember you too well.'

'Hey, Brodie. Remember "Twinkle, Twinkle, Little Star"?' I used to sing it to him at bedtime when I saw him every day after coming off the ice. As I started to softly sing the first couple of lines, he slowly lifted his head and turned to me with a smile which was tentative at first but soon blossomed into pure joy. My beautiful little boy remembered me. That one moment erased the pain of every crossed-out date on my prison calendar.

***

AFTER SIGNING in at Werribee Corrections, Vic and I drove to the boarding house in the western suburb of St Albans. The first four weeks' rent, at $190 a week, was covered by my Centrelink payment. We had to check the address twice, because the house looked more like an ice den than the first stop on the road to recovery. Same tattered sofa on the porch, same line of battered vehicles down the drive, same empty stubbies strewn over the front yard. Vic seemed uncomfortable. He was probably thinking he couldn't leave his kid brother there. But I knew there was a line that couldn't be crossed. He'd already fronted $20,000 in lawyers' fees for my court cases, which was above and beyond any brotherly obligation. I couldn't ask him to put me before his own family by asking to stay at his place.

'Well, this is it,' he said hesitantly. 'I'll wait here until you get your keys.'

I knocked and the door was opened by a creature from another world. Her face looked like a popped balloon, slipping off her head. What used to be a dressing gown was held together by a couple of resilient threads, ready to snap under pressure from her cleavage. She fixed me with one eye while the other wandered all over the neighbourhood. The old crone was clearly smashed out of her head on heroin. I recognised the symptoms immediately.

'It's Simon Fenech,' I said. 'I've been told I have a room here.'

'Come on in, darl,' she drawled. Her breath stank of dead cats. 'They said you were coming. Your room's down the hallway, right opposite mine. If you ever need anything, and I mean anything, just give me a knock, okay?' One eye winked – I think.

She led me down the hallway, past four closed doors, and showed me the shower and the kitchen. The ball of matted hair in the bottom of the shower could well have been a dead rat for all I knew. The kitchen was buried somewhere under the rubble of stubbies and empty takeaway containers.

'Now, darl, this is your room. Promise me you'll lock up, even if you're going for a shower. Nothing's safe in here.' There were five separate bolts on the door, each with an industrial strength padlock. 'One more thing I should tell you,' she croaked, struggling for breath as she bent down to open the bottom locks. 'The bloke in the room next door has a few, ah, mental problems. He pisses against his wall, which is why your room smells a bit of . . .'

The stench as she opened the door bent me double. I retched and thought I was going to spew. The wallpaper was wet and peeling. There was a mattress, complete with a blood stain as big as a family-size pizza. Not a stitch of bedding. Next to the mattress was a bedside table with two of the three drawers missing, and a lamp with no bulb. Three used syringes lay on the floor. Any hope of a new start shrivelled in an instant. All my new-found dignity disappeared. *What the holy fuck? I can't spend one night in this cesspit, never mind four weeks.* I was prepared to face challenges on the outside, but nothing like this. This place was not fit for cockroaches. How could anyone, especially vulnerable ex-offenders with nowhere to go and nothing to their name, be subjected to this? Was it any wonder that so many went straight back to drugs or crime? Vic had to see this, to know that I wasn't exaggerating. He took one look at the room and, covering his nose and mouth with one hand and taking photos on his phone with the other, mumbled, 'Let's get you out of here, brother.'

CHAPTER **NINETEEN**

OCTOBER IN Melbourne can be vindictive. Just as spring tantalises with heartening bursts of warmth, it can just as quickly slap you in the face with an icy blast off the Southern Ocean. The first day in my new lodgings was one such day. I'd virtually begged for the room in a new, clean, nine-bedroom boarding house in Point Cook. For the previous three nights Michelle let me sleep on her couch, a big gesture because it went down like a lead balloon with her boyfriend. Putting Brodie to bed was precious, but I knew that I'd soon out-stayed my welcome.

My problem was that I had no alternative. There was no way I was going back to that cesspit in St Albans, so I turned up at Yarra Housing at 9 a.m. sharp the next day to see what else was available. If you weren't in the first five in the queue, you were sent home. And the queue was a mile long by 9 a.m. I was so desperate for my own place that I made sure that I was first in line the next day, arriving at 7 a.m. It paid off, because the vacancy at Point Cook had just come up. When I told them that I was sleeping in a friend's car, I was bumped to the top of the priority list. The next hurdle was money. The owner wanted a month's deposit, which the housing department stumped up, but I had to pay $380 for the first two weeks' rent up front. All my Centrelink money had been spent on the St Albans cesspit and it would take weeks, months even, to get a refund, especially because Vic had lodged a formal complaint. For a while it looked as though I was going to miss out on the new room, until my wonderful, caring brother stepped up once again.

'You'll never truly know how much this means to me,' I told him. 'That's the last cent I'll ever borrow from you. I swear I'll pay it all back when I'm back on my feet.'

'The best way to repay me is to stay off that shit and show me the brother I once knew,' he replied, before leaving me to settle in.

I had my charity clothes from prison, $66 on my ATM card and a doona which Michelle had loaned me. I needed sheets and a pillowcase, a toothbrush, washing powder and some food. The other occupants of the boarding house were actually quite welcoming. One bloke warned me that the nearest supermarket was a fair hike down the road and offered to lend me his pushbike. Having not been on a bike since I was fourteen, I wobbled to the shops and filled two plastic bags with the essentials, leaving me with thirty cents in my pocket. My food shop consisted of a bag of pasta, a can of tomatoes, an onion, a can of tuna, some chilli flakes, a jar of coffee, a carton of UHT milk, a loaf of bread and a few other essentials. I couldn't wait to cook up the tuna and pasta, with big chunks of oily fish and crunchy, sweet onion – just like Mum made it. But the ride home was going to be a tough slog with the shopping bags balanced on the handlebars and my prison paunch weighing me down even further. As I climbed onto the bike, the skies darkened ominously and a sudden October squall drenched me to the skin, making balancing even more precarious. A few hundred metres along the road I hit a pothole and one of the bags stuck between the spokes of the front wheel, almost throwing me over the top. The bag of pasta burst and time slowed to a stop as my precious can of tuna rolled underneath the wheels of a passing car. *Nooooo* . . . The tuna was crushed. I was crushed. Shivering with cold, I scooped up a handful of sodden pasta and rescued my onion from the gutter. *Hey, nobody said this was going to be easy.*

***

FOR THE first time in my life I literally had no money other than my fortnightly dole payments. The very fact that I was dependent on welfare was humiliating. My days were mostly filled with community service, once again painting over graffiti on overpasses, factory walls and home fences. I had a long list of regular meetings to attend, too, with my corrections case officer, drug and alcohol counsellor and various mental health professionals. This meant more embarrassing bike rides, now on a pushbike borrowed from Michelle's ten-year-old son, which was three sizes too small. Was I being paranoid? Or were old associates sniggering as the big-shot kickboxing drug dealer huffed and puffed his way past them? Were familiar faces from the local constabulary sneering, triumphant at reducing a former adversary to such a pitiful state? No, paranoia was a thing of the past.

My evenings were spent alone, in front of a crappy TV that I'd picked up from a hard rubbish collection on the side of the road. A solid purple line filled the centre of the screen so, unless I was watching tennis with both players either side of this LCD net, most programs were hard to follow. One highlight, every second week, was receiving my food parcel from the Uniting Church and checking to see if there was any fresh fruit or vegetables.

I needed work and I told the Salvation Army employment agency that I was prepared to do anything, washing dishes or picking up dog shit, whatever. I was smoking like a chimney and it was burning a hole in my meagre budget. Invariably, when employers found out I was an ex-con, the doors slammed shut. When they learnt about my back injury, they were spineless. If any of them did manage to see past these barriers, the stringent corrections order obligations meant that I lost their commitment. An alternative to finding a job would've been to chase all my old debts, which ran into tens of thousands of dollars. During my time in jail every single one of my old toys and cars had gone missing. But that course of action would've inevitably led back to jail, or death. I was even forced to kiss goodbye to the two forty-foot containers filled with legitimate car parts, all stripped, labelled and packaged up, when the farmer in Melton sold his land and told me to remove my stuff or lose it. I had no licence, no mates to call on and nowhere to store what could've been my ticket to stability.

I was slipping back into depression. Realistically, what hope did any ex-offender who wanted to put their past behind them have of turning over a new leaf when the odds were stacked against us? What about the men who'd served much longer sentences, known as boobheads, who'd become institutionalised and had no clue how to cope in the modern world? Was it any wonder that so many found themselves back in jail so quickly?

Yet I was never once tempted to return to ice. My resolve was indestructible, driven by the dream to be a real father to my kids again. Brodie knew no different, but I'd been out of Jake's and Mackenzie's lives for too long. Did I have a right to disrupt their stable family life with Vicky and their stepdad, Paul, at my own convenience? I didn't know the answer to that question but I actually felt that I had a lot to offer. So I pleaded my case with Vicky. Then, one week before Christmas, I received the best present imaginable. After eighteen months without any contact, Mackenzie wanted to see me.

I arranged to meet them at The Pancake Parlour in Werribee Plaza, Mackenzie's favourite. Man, I was nervous. I scoured the op shops for something decent to wear – a black Everlast T-shirt and some new trackie bottoms – and treated myself to a new $5 beard trimmer. I also bought her a kit for making dolls' clothes for Christmas. Mum and daughter arrived hand in hand and Mackenzie looked so grown up, a gorgeous young lady. I wanted to squeeze her so hard, but I sensed I had to take it slow. She seemed a little bashful, as though she was checking whether this was really her dad. Vicky said that it was good to see me looking more like my old self, then she left us alone.

'Right, let's order,' I said, rubbing my hands together. It was a treat for me, too. 'I'll have the Jamaican banana hotcakes and, if I remember rightly, you'll have the triple stack with hot chocolate fudge?'

'Actually, can I have the Mexican beef crepes?' *She really has grown up*, I thought.

'You bet. Here, this is your Christmas present. It's not much, though. I don't have a whole lot of money at the moment. You can open it now if you like.'

Mackenzie stifled a chuckle when she tore off the paper. 'Thanks, Dad. But you know I'm twelve years old now, right? I haven't played with dolls for years.'

'Yeah, right, what a dumbarse. We've got a lot of catching up to do. I'm guessing Jake won't be wanting this Lego, either.'

Mackenzie went silent, dropping her gaze to the table. 'Actually, I'm not sure Jake will want anything from you. He's still pretty upset about everything.'

'I wondered why he didn't come with you. I just want a chance to tell you both how much I love you and try to explain how sick I've been. That man wasn't your dad. And I'm going to make it up to you both. From now on I'm going to be the best dad possible.'

'Okay, I'll tell him. But he won't listen.'

Mackenzie, on the other hand, hung on my every word. She was fascinated by prison, and wanted to know all about her half-brother, Brodie. She was worried that I was living on my own and suggested that I might be able to go to their house for Christmas dinner.

Slowly the same adoring look that she'd had as a three year old, when her dad was her ultimate hero, returned. *God, I love this girl*, I told myself. How I stopped myself from breaking down I'll never know, but I didn't want her to think that I was a nut job. The hour flew by and, when Vicky returned, Mackenzie flung her arms around me and hugged me with a conviction that said 'my dad's back'. It was quite possibly *the* most powerful moment in my life. I could conquer any adversity if that was the prize.

***

HUNGER – genuine, aching hunger – was a new experience for me. Unable to break the grip of nicotine addiction, cutting my food bill was the only way to pay my rent. Apart from visits with Mackenzie and Brodie, I lived like a hermit, fulfilling my corrections order obligations by day and staying home at night. Even when I finally got my driver's licence back, there was little prospect of a job that would break me out of the poverty trap.

'I'm losing hope here,' I told my corrections case worker, a sulky girl in her twenties whose own job satisfaction was measured by boxes ticked, not meaningful assistance. 'Something's got to give. I literally can't carry on like this. There's no chance of getting back on my feet if all these stupid obligations, which I've already completed five times over, stop me from getting a job. I'm going to be honest with you. I'm hungry and right now I feel like my only option is to start dealing drugs again. Is that what you guys want? So you can lock me up again?' There was some truth in this. Although I would never have taken ice again, it would've been easy to chase down a couple of debts and hit up Speed Dial for a one-off score. At times it was truly tempting, but who was I trying to kid? There's no such thing as a one-off deal in ice land. The smallest step back in that direction would have been disastrous. But I could certainly understand why so many in my shoes succumbed. When you feel that society has abandoned you, why respect its rules? What incentive is there to fight for yourself if it feels like it's you against the world?

'So you want a job, right?' she said, barely awake. I felt like screaming, *Yes! I've been telling you that for fucking months.* 'Um, I think I saw something this morning. Maybe I threw the leaflet away.' She reached underneath her desk and un-scrunched a leaflet from a company called Fruit2Work. 'Yeah, this is the one. They need a driver for two shifts a week to deliver fruit to offices. And they want someone with an offending background.' *And you threw the leaflet away…?*

A few days later in a café, I met with an elegant, sophisticated lady called Coral, who was on a counselling placement at Fruit2Work. The company had been set up by two youngish guys who were involved with the Foundation for Young Australians. One was a psychiatrist at Barwon Prison, frustrated that so many ex-cons soon returned to jail because of a lack of job or housing opportunities. The idea, to employ ex-offenders to deliver fruit to companies and organisations in the CBD while preparing them for full-time work, was simple and proved to be a great example of a social enterprise, a business that addresses a community need. Soon Fruit2Work was too big for them to handle and was sold to Whitelion, a youth charity that already ran several other social enterprises.

Coral was a sympathetic listener and teared up at several points in my life story. When I finished pouring my heart out, a well-dressed guy who was sitting further along our communal table stood up and tentatively approached. 'I hope you don't mind me interrupting, but I couldn't help overhearing,' he said. 'You, sir, are an inspiration. Here I was, feeling sorry for myself and dreading work this morning. You put everything into perspective. If you can overcome what you've had to deal with, then I'm quite sure I can cope with a few little hiccups. I do hope you get the job. Here's my card in case I can help in any way in the future.' Turned out this bloke was one of the top executives at the Reserve Bank of Australia! It was an epiphany. *If I can touch people and inspire them to do better at work and home, then perhaps some good can come out of everything that has happened.*

Coral was impressed that I'd made such an impact and offered me the job on the spot, starting at 2 a.m. the next Monday. I was elated.

It was pissing down outside when I woke up the next morning, but I felt like Gene Kelly in *Singing in the Rain*. There was a spring in my step, until I spotted a homeless guy scrabbling around on all fours looking for sodden cigarette butts.

'Here mate,' I told him and handed over my full packet. 'This one's on me.'

***

REACHING THAT first rung on the ladder was crucial. Someone had shown faith in me and I wasn't going to let them down. But how the hell was I supposed to get to Epping Market, fifty kilometres from where I was staying, at two in the morning? I would've crawled there if necessary, or taken three or four trains and waited on a park bench, but once again my hero, Vic, helped me out by loaning me $500 to buy a clapped-out Mitsubishi Lancer. I saved enough money for half a tank of petrol and filled up at the servo opposite Werribee police station. While I was at the pump, a patrol car pulled up and an officer who had arrested me on a couple of occasions approached.

'What you up to, Fenech?' he asked.

'On my way to work.'

'Yeah, righto! Do you even have a licence?'

'Yep, it's here. Don't make me late, eh?'

He checked my licence and radioed through to find out whether the car was registered.

'All seems in order. How much ice have you had tonight?'

'Nothing. I'm clean. You won't ever find me with that shit again.'

'Heard that before,' he scoffed. 'Why don't we do a quick drug test?'

'Yeah, no problem,' I said. The cop's face fell when the test was negative. 'Told ya. I'm clean. There's no fucking way I'm going back to jail.'

'I suppose there's a first for everything,' he said, deflated. Another easy arrest, another pointless statistic, had been denied him. 'But I won't hold my breath,' he added.

***

PULLING ON a hi-viz shirt for the first time in ages felt empowering. I was valued again, earning, worthy of respect. Packing the fruit boxes for that morning's delivery run, alongside the supervisor and a rich kid who had been heading down the path of ice addiction, might have seemed menial to some. But every apple, orange and banana felt precious to me; nutrition for a new life. Soon I was driving Fruit2Work's Toyota HiAce van on delivery runs and was allowed to take it home. I handed out leftover fruit to the homeless like Robin Hood, although many turned their noses up at this alien nourishment. I was trusted with a credit card for fuel, and allowed into the empty offices of major corporations before their staff arrived for work in the morning. Office workers greeted me with a smile and a chat. I was Simon the Fruit Guy, not Simon the ex-con junkie.

Okay, so I broke one small promise. I'd assured Vic that I would pay him back for the car with every spare cent from my first pay packets. But my jocks, the same two pairs I hand-scrubbed in prison, had disintegrated into baggy, threadbare nappies. So I treated myself to two new pairs, and a new pair of socks. (Plus a Hungry Jack's double whopper with cheese.) After that I paid Vic back in three weeks. There was fresh incentive to clear my community service as quickly as possible, too, so that I could take another part-time job building fences for Vicky's partner, Paul, a former prison guard who had been a great stepdad to Jake and Mackenzie.

When my corrections order commitments were finally completed, there was enough money in my account to pay for some dental work. Sure, my teeth had been weakened by the acidic ice smoke eating away at the enamel for all those years, and my gums were eroded, but I still felt sore that the cops had used unnecessary force when they slammed me into the pavement. Three new caps and one replacement tooth cost $800 but I at last could talk again without self-consciously looking down at the floor. I had a smile back on my face, and in my heart.

As Fruit2Work grew, so did my responsibility. I became the supervisor of a team of eight men and women, some who'd already been to jail and some who were on the precipice. Most had kids. Could my own experiences help any of these people, who had been shunted off to the wastelands of society, to stay out of jail and become better parents? Without decent role models, what hope did their children have of staying drug and crime free? Many charities and agencies focused on support for young offenders and addicts, but few addressed the needs of older generations.

For instance, one of our employees, Billy, was living in housing commission with his pregnant partner and in constant trouble with the law. I saw a spark of potential and bought his lunch for two weeks out of my own pocket to make sure that he stayed with us for long enough to make a difference. I even accompanied him to court to explain his progress. He now has a full-time job, lives in a rented house and is bringing up a son who has a chance of a better start to life than his father. Another bloke, Jono, in his early thirties, stole to fund a chronic gambling addiction. He'd never had a father figure in his life. Nobody knew the importance of that role model more than I did, so I took him under my wing and coached him towards a job driving forklifts.

'We're a social enterprise, not a charity,' I told him. 'We need to make a profit so that we can help more people like you. And if you're half an hour late for your deliveries, then that's lost revenue. Smarten yourself up, too. You're representing our company. Take pride in your appearance. Tomorrow, have a shower and put on a clean shirt before coming in, please.'

Not earth-shattering life lessons, but nobody had ever taken the trouble to teach him the basics of holding down a job. Then there was Locky, not much younger than me, who'd been jailed for ice-related offences and was banned from seeing his kids when he got out. Again, my own experiences were invaluable in helping him overturn the court order and become a part of his kids' lives again. A few months after he left us to take up a job driving tilt-trays, he sent me a poolside picture from a holiday with his older boy and girl, and their new baby brother.

Our influence on the life of that man, and many others, was immeasurable.

Not every story has a happy ending, though. Rick's demise broke my heart. He was a heroin addict of thirty-five years, all skin and bones but with a very sharp brain. The placement at Fruit2Work was his last chance saloon and I was happy to start my shifts early so that I could give him a lift from Werribee to Epping. Otherwise, he would have lapsed, for sure. By then I'd moved out of my room at Point Cook and into a room in Bluey's old home in Birdsville, commonly known as the Bronx.

Although Bluey's partner, Doreen, was clean, she was struggling to cope after his death and my rent came in very handy. Here, there was even more reason to keep myself to myself. I wanted nothing to do with anyone in that area and, when I finally found my feet financially, took the first chance to move out into the country, to a small town called Romsey in the Macedon Ranges. For the same money I could rent an entire house, and I immediately felt at home. The air was fresh. Nights were siren-free. People were trustworthy. I had no history there and could enjoy a Sunday morning coffee in the local café without dirty looks or filthy gossip. I found head space, for the first time in a long time. The drawback was that I could no longer offer Rick a ride to work. And without that job, he was almost certain to return to drugs. I couldn't let that happen.

'Come and live with me in Romsey,' I suggested. 'There's a spare room in the house. I'll be glad of the company.'

'I can't do that, mate,' he said. 'You value your own space. And what about Zeus?' Rick lived for his dog, a blue healer–kelpie cross.

'Bring her with you, no problem.' I'd eventually lost my battle to have Axel returned, despite an appeal to the Supreme Court through an organisation called Pets on Trial. I tried not to think where my beautiful boy had ended up, but I knew the healing properties of a pet all too well.

Rick looked at me with absolute incredulity. 'I'm a bit lost for words. Nobody's showed me kindness like that for a long time.'

'Shut the fuck up before I start blubbering,' I said and laughed. 'Pack your stuff tonight.'

Rick was in his element in Romsey. He took Zeus for walks into the bush and we chatted long into the nights about our experiences. Gradually, he rebuilt bridges with his kids. And then, after his first nine months free of heroin for thirty-five years, he was diagnosed with liver cancer. The deterioration was rapid and we had no choice but to move him closer to his family for specialist care. At the funeral his family told me of their appreciation at having the real Rick back for those precious weeks before his death. I was proud to help carry his coffin. How I loved that man.

***

BEFORE LONG I was promoted again to operations manager when Fruit2Work boss Rob Brown, a larger-than-life Scotsman who had turned his back on a high-flying corporate career to concentrate on helping others, spotted my potential to make more of an impact, and not just in our company. Just as I became a mentor to many of our employees, Rob nurtured my raw business skills and gently encouraged me to use my experiences as a force for good by delivering talks and presentations. It wasn't always easy to open up in front of strangers. The easy way would've been to try to bury my past. But speaking honestly was cathartic, a way of anchoring myself in achievement rather than failure. I spoke in boardrooms about the dangers of ice, I spoke on construction sites about the importance of work safety, and I spoke in jails about staying out of prison. The effect during my talks was always the same: you could hear a pin drop. My story resonated with audiences from all walks of life.

**

'DAD, I'M so proud of you,' said Mackenzie when I told her that I'd been selected as one of three finalists for the Social Enterprise Champion of the Year award. We were back at Werribee Plaza during one of my regular weekend visits.

'You have no idea how much it means to me to hear those words, sweetheart,' I said. 'Do you think Jakey will ever think that way?'

'Give it time,' she said, with a wisdom beyond her years. 'He's been very angry. At first he didn't want anyone to even mention your name. He's not like that now, but I think he's worried that if he lets you back into his life, you might let him down again.'

Jake's rejection was hard to accept. My redemption seemed

incomplete without my son's blessing. Just then, I spotted the copper who had drug-tested me at the servo on my first night at Fruit2Work. He was strolling purposefully towards us with a dumb grin on his face. I wanted to duck into the nearest shop to avoid him. *No, fuck that. I've got nothing to hide from this prick,* I thought.

'Ah, Fenech, we meet again,' he said, blocking our path. 'And who's this young lady, then?'

'This is Mackenzie, my daughter. We're just doing a bit of shopping.'

'No worries, I'm not here to cause drama. Just wanted to say that I actually looked you up the other day. There are no new charges on file since you came out. I haven't heard your name mentioned around the station, either.'

'I told you before, I'm never going back to that shit.'

'And good on ya. To be honest, I thought you'd never come good. But you're unrecognisable from the man I first arrested. Just goes to show, there's hope for everyone who's addicted to that stuff. Mackenzie, I reckon your old man's going to be okay.'

'I *know* he is,' she said, grabbing my hand and dragging me away.

EPILOGUE

TO DREAM that love might enter my life once again was an indulgence I rarely permitted myself in prison. During the ice years, love had been inaccessible, locked tightly away behind conflicting needs and fleeting desires. Freedom provided the chance to start afresh. I had an ideal partner in mind – someone with inner beauty. I was done with show ponies. I convinced myself I was more likely to find her in the country than in the rat race of the city, but she certainly wasn't going to waltz into my life while I was delivering fruit at 3 a.m.

Online dating was the answer. But how was I going to summarise my life in a Tinder profile? *Single male, mid-forties, carrying a few extra kilos, two failed marriages, multiple knife wound scars, former drug addict, just out of jail* . . . There's an invitation to swipe left. I wanted to be honest, though. There was no time for playing games. So I opted for: *Divorcee, loving father of three, been around the tracks but now looking for someone genuine and humble to share a new hope.*

The first couple of dates were disappointing, devoid of emotional connection. Then I was contacted by Jasmine, a pharmacy assistant from Kangaroo Flat, about an hour's drive from Romsey. Her Tinder experiences had been equally fruitless and she was in the process of deleting her profile when I popped up on her screen. We swapped messages for a few weeks and arranged a date at Soltan Pepper, the best restaurant in Romsey – and quite possibly the world! When Jasmine walked through the door, fashionably fifteen minutes late, my stomach went nuts, and not because I was starving. Inner beauty would've been a bonus, because the outer beauty was just fine. Glossy shoulder-length dark hair framed a warm, pretty face which hinted at an endearing shyness and vulnerability. Is it too clichéd to say that I instantly knew she was the one? Well, I don't care, because it was true. There were none of the usual awkward formal opening exchanges. We were instantly on the same wavelength.

'I'll order the Thai curry served on *jasmine* rice,' I told the waiter, 'because *jasmine* is my favourite.'

'That is so corny,' she said, laughing. 'I was going to order the pork belly because it came from a fat pig!'

'Well, fuck you,' I said, matter-of-factly. We pissed ourselves laughing. Before the evening was finished Jasmine knew my life story. I learnt that she'd suffered her own fair share of troubles, too. We were both ready to start the healing process.

Jazz was mother to three girls. Bonnie and Bree were both in their twenties and had left home, but eight-year-old Addison still lived with her mum – and lived for her mum. Bonnie and Bree were quick to welcome me, as were Jazz's parents. With Addy we were more cautious. But the more she heard about Simon, the more she wanted to meet him. She was adorable, a mini version of her mum. Though wary at first, her defences quickly crumbled. Before long, Addy wouldn't go anywhere unless she was on my shoulders. My dream of new start, a million miles from the horrors of my past, was starting to take shape.

***

PICTURE THIS scene, please. It's nearly two years since I met Jazz, a sun-kissed Saturday afternoon in the backyard of our rented home in Kyneton. I'm cooking up a magnificent barbecue, if I say so myself – only the best burgers, steaks and snags from the best local producers. A clean, warm breeze drifts over from the Macedon Ranges and wafts the aromas towards our guests – my beautiful family.

There's Vic, on his second glass of shiraz and chuckling away with his wife, Kerine. He glances frequently over to the barbie. He's a Fenech, after all, and loves a feed. My love and admiration for that man knows no bounds. How many times did his faith in me hold strong against all the odds? How many times did he go above and beyond the obligations of brotherhood? By loaning me rent money for a decent place to stay after being released from prison, Vic cut through the chains that drag so many back into a life of reoffending. Recently, I paid back all the money I owed him, around $20,000, a very meaningful moment for me. But I still owe him everything.

There's Mackenzie, joyfully pushing Brodie on the swing at the bottom of the lawn. Recently, Mackenzie and I went for a spa day together – manicure, pedicure, eyebrows, the works.

And she offered to help pay for it out of her own pocket money, realising that money was tight approaching Christmas. How many fourteen year olds would be so selfless and considerate? This girl has a truly wonderful soul. Her grandparents would have been proud. And there's Brodie; bouncy, boisterous Brodie. A real chip off the old block. I'll be watching you like a hawk, my boy. Let me guide you gently away from temptation. For now, my son doesn't know how to frown or slow down.

Addy joins in the fun on the swing. She's besotted with her stepbrother. I love this girl like my own daughter. Earlier this week she chased me down the driveway on my way to work. She wanted to kiss me goodbye. She tells me she loves me every day. Can life get any more precious? The new Axel bounds over to the kids. Until now he's been way too interested in the meat on the barbie and, anyway, he rarely leaves my side. He reminds me of the old Axel in so many ways – the same markings, the same shape, the same sooky nature. I just hope the original, wherever he might be, is as content as his doggy doppelganger.

Addy's sisters and their partners are chatting with my boss, Rob, and his wife, Linda. It's a rare thing to want to invite your boss into your own home. But it's a privilege to know and learn from this man. He's dressed to impress, as always, and is in the middle of a long (and loud) story. But there'll be a lesson in there, so listen well, guys. If more high-achievers like Rob were willing to sacrifice personal gain and use their talents for the greater good, we'd be able to keep many more people out of jail and at home with their families.

Rob is proud – as am I – that not one man or woman who has been through the Fruit2Work program has gone back inside.

Around the country, almost every other prisoner returns to jail within two years. That's unacceptable when programs like ours can achieve so much. Think of the huge savings that could be made if more investment was made in social enterprises and more companies and organisations bought their services. That's the commercial argument. But we see the human impact, which is much more important.

Earlier in the week I was Santa at the Fruit2Work Christmas party. Many of our old employees came with their kids. I knew all their faces because my office wall is covered with pictures of happy families that've been held together with the glue of new opportunity. It's how I rationalise this whole story. I only survived my grief, my trauma, my addiction and my life of crime because God wants me to help others. The tougher the apprenticeship, the more influential the teacher.

Don't get me wrong, my redemption isn't always plain sailing. Just this week I attended Addy's school Christmas concert. The pure innocence of so many young souls was overpowering. What place did I have in a setting of such hope? I felt I had no right to taint this occasion with my baggage. In that moment, I was disgusted with myself. Tears of self-pity flowed silently. Then Addy came on stage. The same tears continued to flow, but from a fresh source. I snapped out of the self-loathing and took pride in the role model I had become.

Regret will never be far away. Often, I look back on the past decade and recoil in horror at the things I did and the choices I made. Was that really me? Was one puff of ice all it took to send my life into freefall? No, of course not. I have to take responsibility for my actions. I could have stopped taking drugs at any time.

I should never have dealt. I was reckless with my disregard for societal boundaries. But anyone who has been strangled by this vicious drug will know that its grip is unrelenting. It feeds off ever-increasing weakness, a parasite on frailty. The mind is merely a poisoned host. And we are talking hundreds and hundreds of thousands of lives being destroyed, here in Australia and around the world. It devastates whole communities, especially in rural areas. It's out of control in some Indigenous populations, among young people and LGBTQI groups. And trust me, the quoted figures are underestimates, because this drug flourishes in the shadows.

I was fortunate. My last remaining family member stood by me. Vic never lost sight of hope. Many do lose hope, though, because ice sorely tests family bonds and friendships. It usually falls on outside agencies to intervene. And in my mind that should mean compulsory rehabilitation, not prison; restoration, not punishment. Voluntary measures, such as counselling and mental health support, are well-meaning but ineffective. Investment in the kind of residential rehab facilities that are needed is negligible compared to the scale of the epidemic. Perhaps my story can help to make a difference. Then being so painfully honest will have been worthwhile.

There's a gaping hole in this otherwise perfect family celebration. My son Jake's not here. I haven't spoken to my son since before I went to prison, when I was newly off the ice and felt justified in attempting to re-enter his life. He didn't want to see me then, still too angry at having been abandoned for a drug. I couldn't blame him then and cannot blame him now. One day, I pray, I'll have the chance to put my arm around his shoulder and explain that addiction is a disease. Convince him that the man who was such a pitiful father is transformed. Until that day I'll rejoice in what I have, not what I have lost.

A slender arm reaches around my shoulder and the sun explodes off the gold of Jazz's engagement ring. I told you she was the one! I flip the burgers and steaks, put down the spatula and our lips touch.

'Have you already had one of those sausages?' she says and laughs. Except where food is concerned, our trust is absolute. The two years together have been everything I dreamt of from my prison bunk. Jazz has a radiant inner beauty. She'll do anything for anyone, like delivering medicines to elderly customers on her own time, or dressing their wounds at home. She used to work four jobs to provide for her daughters. Now she dotes on Brodie and is like a big sister to Mackenzie. She knows when to let me disappear into my own thoughts, and when a reassuring touch is all that is needed. And she expects nothing in return. So I'm glad to have dinner on the table for her when she comes home from work, to stroll hand in hand along the banks of the Campaspe River at the weekend, or to surprise her with a trip to Soltan Pepper, to say nothing more than 'thanks'. Thanks for judging me for the man I am today, and not the man I once was.

ABOUT Fruit2Work

FRUIT2WORK STARTED in 2017 and was certified as a social enterprise business in 2018. We deliver fruit and dairy products to workplaces, creating chances for those exiting the justice system who typically wouldn't be given the opportunity due to their backgrounds.

The core social issue that Fruit2Work seeks to address is our State's unacceptable level of recidivism, or the rate of re-offending. Victoria has a recidivism rate of 44 per cent within two years of release – one of the highest rates in the world – creating a huge social and financial burden on society. It's a travesty, given Melbourne's label as one of the world's most liveable cities.

In simple financial terms, for every person we have helped to stay out of the justice system, the saving is at least $250,000 per year to the taxpayer. In its three years of operation, nobody who has participated in the Fruit2Work program has returned to the justice system — ZERO recidivism – a remarkable statistic that is among the best in the world.

We are often asked: 'So what is the magic?' Well, Simon Fenech is one of the magicians who helps make it happen.

Credibility and empathy (not sympathy) are two key ingredients in the success of Fruit2Work. Simon's story clearly articulates why he has these characteristics in spades.

There are other ingredients, too: being willing to suspend judgement; speaking the same language as participants; recognising that our past doesn't define our future; believing that stigma can be overcome; and agreeing that we all deserve to be treated with respect and dignity. These principles are easy to write about but much more difficult to live and breathe on a daily basis. That, however, is what defines the culture and magic of Fruit2Work.

We are not a team of do-gooders, though. We hold each other to account, occasionally dishing out some tough love, but in a way that respects each other and the journey that we travel.

On a personal note, as much as Simon may hint at me being some sort of mentor and grey-haired sage, the fact is that Simon inspires me every day by the way in which he continues to positively change his own life and the lives of others. The lessons he has learned are now having a ripple effect through the various audiences he reaches.

For more details about Fruit2Work, please contact: accounts@ fruit2work.com.au.

Rob Brown
CEO of Fruit2Work

ACKNOWLEDGEMENTS

TO NEIL BRAMWELL, for bringing my story to life and for treating it with compassion, courtesy and respect. It was written as though he was there with me every step of the way and I value the friendship we've developed. To Rob Brown, owner of Fruit2Work, who has encouraged me to share my story and has been an amazing mentor. To Benny and the Echo team for believing in this book and its message. I would also like to thank my partner Jasmine for re-living my story without judgement.

Simon Fenech

SHARING SIMON'S pain and joy has been a privilege and I thank him for his unflinching honesty, without which no book of this nature is possible. He continues to educate me as a true friend. Benny, Tegan and the team at Echo have been a joy to work with, not forgetting Angela. And a huge thanks to Team Bramwell – Martine, Teddy and Albert (the dog) – for their constant support and adoration!

Neil Bramwell

ABOUT THE AUTHORS

SIMON FENECH is the operations manager of the social enterprise Fruit2Work,
which creates meaningful employment
opportunities for those who are impacted
by the justice system by delivering fresh
fruit and milk to workplaces. A former
Australian and South Pacific kickboxing
champion, Simon was a finalist in the Social Enterprise Champion
of the Year award in 2019. He lives with his family in Victoria.

NEIL BRAMWELL is a Melbourne-based
author of numerous books, including
Foggy, the number one bestselling auto-
biography of motorcycle racer Carl Fogarty.
He discovered Simon's inspirational story
when researching a book on social
enterprise in Australia, *Dollars&Sense*.

Discover more gripping true crime from Echo

SHORTLISTED FOR THE 2016 NED KELLY AWARD
FOR BEST TRUE CRIME AND THE
DAVITT AWARD FOR BEST NON-FICTION

THE STING

THE UNDERCOVER
OPERATION
THAT CAUGHT
DANIEL
MORCOMBE'S
KILLER

KATE KYRIACOU

The disappearance of Queensland schoolboy Daniel Morcombe was one of the most confounding child abduction and murder cases of the century. Now read the shocking and extraordinary true story of the police sting that resulted in the confession of Daniel's killer.